# THE GUILT-FREE DOG OWNER'S GUIDE

## Caring for a Dog When You're Short on Time and Space

Diana Delmar

Illustrations by Paté Lawson

A Storey Publishing Book

STOREY

Storey Communications, Inc.
Pownal, Vermont 05261

*To my parents, Bettie and Gene;*
*to my husband, Kerry;*
*and to*
*Beau, Phoenix, and Ferro.*

Cover and text design by Wanda Harper

Cover illustration by Paté Lawson

Edited by Benjamin Watson

*Printed in the United States by Book Press*
*Fifth Printing, July 1991*

**Library of Congress Cataloguing-in-Publication Data**
Delmar, Diana, 1951-
    The guilt-free dog owner's guide : caring for a dog when you're short on time and space / Diana Delmar ; illustrations by Paté Lawson.
        p.      cm.
    "A Storey Publishing book."
    Includes bibliographical references.
    ISBN 0-88266-575-8 (pbk.) : $7.95
    ISBN 0-88266-605-3 : $16.95
    1. Dogs.   I. Title.
SF427.D414   1990                   89-61788
636.7—dc20                       CIP

# CONTENTS

Acknowledgments .........................................5

1 The Dog Choice..........................................7

2 The New Dog in the House......................37

3 The Housebroken Dog............................53

4 The Safe Dog............................................71

5 The Polite Dog .........................................89

6 Dog Schedules, Sitters, and Kennels .....109

7 The Polite Dog Owner...........................119

8 The Groomed Dog..................................125

9 The Fit Dog .............................................137

10 The Doctored Dog................................149

11 The Dog House .....................................167

Product and Information List ..................173

Recommended Reading...........................175

Index .......................................................177

## Acknowledgments

Joseph J. Seneczko, D.V.M., who practices veterinary medicine in the Chicago area, took considerable time from his busy schedule to provide me with information and to review the manuscript.

Three members of the dedicated staff of the Humane Society of the United States likewise patiently answered numerous questions and read over the material: Randall Lockwood, Ph.D., director of higher education programs; Guy Hodge, director of data and information; and Phyllis Wright, vice-president of companion animals.

Stephen Rafe, of Starfire Enterprises in Warrenton, Virginia, an author and behavior communications counselor, provided a wealth of resource information and helpful advice.

I am perhaps most grateful to my friends, who helped with the project in any way they could and were unfailing in their enthusiasm and encouragement.

## CHAPTER 1

# THE DOG CHOICE

*Selecting a Dog for Urban Living*

C ompanionship, compassion. Do you identify with these two words as they relate to dogs? If so, you have the makings of a happy dog owner no matter where you live, even if it's in a row house with a tiny backyard or a high-rise apartment.

Companionship is the primary reason you should want a dog. You should be the kind of person who takes great delight in having the dog curled at your feet or prancing next to you down the sidewalk. The antics of the playful dog stealing a slipper or racing through the house amuse you. Compassion for dogs means that you enjoy nurturing them and that you understand and welcome their dependence on you for their basic needs: food, water, medical attention, safe housing, and loving attention.

There's no question that it can be more difficult to keep a dog in urban or increasingly congested suburban areas than in the country. For one thing, there is usually limited space in and out-of-doors to exercise. In addition, many dog owners tend to be busy people who may have trouble coordinating their schedules with the needs of their dogs. They must go out of their way to be considerate of their neighbors; they must make sure their dog doesn't bark incessantly or lunge at passersby on the street; and they must take care to clean up after their dogs. But does this mean that even urban dwellers should forgo the pleasures of dog ownership? If you really want a dog, and you are willing to accommodate the needs of a dog, the answer is an unequivocal "No."

In many respects, the town or city dog can be healthier and happier than the outdoor country dog. Dogs that live outside, especially if they are allowed to run loose, are more susceptible to injury and disease. They might get caught in a fence, get into scraps with other animals, or be hit by a car or stolen. They are also more likely to play host to parasites and other diseases. These problems are far less likely for the dog that lives in his owner's house and goes outside only on a leash.

Considering that dogs are pack animals who do not like to be alone, dogs living in close proximity with their owners are probably happier than the lone dog roaming the fields or the suburban dog left to entertain himself all day in a backyard.

## Solving the Dog Owner's Problems

Most of the problems that today's urban and suburban dog owners have — limited space, a busy schedule, and cleanup problems — can be easily addressed. The first step is to select a dog compatible with your lifestyle, which you will learn to do in this chapter. The next step involves developing an individualized approach to caring for your dog. To do that you need options — a choice of solutions to your problems, so that you can find remedies that work for you. That's what the rest of the book is about.

Even if you unexpectedly find yourself carrying home a dog without having given much thought to your selection, chances are that you and the dog will have a happy union if you love the dog, and if you are willing to go a little bit out of your way to accommodate the needs of your pet.

## A Quiz for Prospective Dog Owners

This short, semi-serious quiz will help you consider characteristics about yourself that are important regarding dog ownership and will point out some of the pleasures and perils of being a dog owner.

1) You are walking home from the store and a cute, obviously friendly little dog dragging a broken leash follows you. You:
   **a)** ignore the dog.
   **b)** take the dog to the local animal shelter.
   **c)** keep the dog with you and try to find the owner.

2) A guest accidentally spills a drink on your white carpet. You:
   **a)** figure a carpet is to be used and clean it up.
   **b)** are upset and angry.
   **c)** decide to replace the carpet with one that's a more practical color when your budget allows.

3) You adopt a friendly older dog from the local animal shelter. But, after several weeks, the dog is still having accidents in the house and chewing up shoes. You:
   **a)** give the dog back to the shelter.
   **b)** try to figure out why the dog has not adjusted and take action to correct the problem.
   **c)** decide there's nothing you can do and that you have to live with the aggravation.

4) You have company in your living room and your ten-month-old dog comes racing through with your underwear in her mouth. You:
    **a)** think it's funny.
    **b)** put your underwear in a place the dog can't get to.
    **c)** are angry at the dog and embarrassed.

5) You have paper-trained your dog, but he "goes" on newspaper that was left on top of the coffee table! You:
    **a)** punish the dog.
    **b)** clean it up, say nothing to the dog, but watch where you leave the paper the next time you go out.
    **c)** tell the dog "No" and show him the paper in the storage room he's supposed to use.

*See end of chapter for answers.*

## Your Personality and Lifestyle

When you go about selecting a dog, be sure to think about the kind of lifestyle you and your family *presently* lead, not the kind you would *like* to lead. This will help prevent you from developing unrealistic expectations of your ability to meet a dog's needs. Next, think ahead. If your lifestyle is likely to change in the future, can you incorporate those changes with your selection of a dog? For instance, if you don't have children now but might in the future, consider a dog of a breed that's known for getting along well with children.

### You

Take an honest look at the kind of person you are. First and foremost, dog owners should be reliable and committed persons who believe that a dog and owner live together "until death do they part."

Now look at your energy level and envision yourself with a dog. Are you more likely to be reading, with a dog curled at your feet, or taking energetic walks and romping in the park with your pet? Chances are that if you don't like long walks now, you won't like them any better just because you have a dog that has to be walked a lot. But a breed of dog that can satisfy most of its exercise requirements romping in the house could be a happy addition to your life. On the other hand, if you're the outdoorsy type who enjoys long, vigorous jaunts around the neighborhood, you aren't going to be happy with an English bulldog that cannot tolerate great amounts of exercise.

If you prefer a quiet home life, don't select a dog known for being a particularly active breed, although almost all puppies are going to run around a lot, regardless of breed.

Are you a zombie in the morning? If you can't stand the idea of having to take a dog outside before you have your first cup of coffee, then you had better select a dog that can be trained to permanently use papers or a box indoors.

You also need to consider your physical attributes. If you lack muscular strength, you won't want a dog with the power to drag you down the block.

## Your Family

Make certain that everyone in your home really wants a dog. It almost goes without saying that, if there's someone in the house who doesn't like dogs and is intolerant of them, you should forgo dog ownership. The ideal situation is a household in which there is one reliable person who wants to take responsibility for the majority of dog care, and other people in the house who want to help.

Besides considering a dog breed's compatibility with children, don't forget the elderly — if you have senior citizens in your home, you will want to get a breed known for gentleness, not a boisterous breed that's hard to handle and could knock people over, especially since most dogs live in close proximity to their owners. However, the presence of children or senior citizens is reason enough to get a dog. A dog provides wonderful companionship for children and the elderly alike. Small children, properly guided by their parents, learn to value companionship and learn about responsibility by having a dog. It has also been said that, for teenagers, the loyal, loving attention dogs give helps to build self-esteem.

For people of all ages, dogs not only provide companionship but also physical benefits. Petting a dog is known to lower blood pressure, which may in turn help counter stress. Dogs are increasingly being used to help draw out isolated nursing home patients and depressed people of all ages. And we've all heard the heartwarming true stories of dogs who guide the blind through busy city streets, hear for the deaf, and fetch for people who are paralyzed.

Many people find that dogs provide a way to meet other people. Dog owners walking down the street are far more likely to stop and converse than people without a dog because it's immediately apparent that they have something in common.

## Your Schedule

If, like many city dwellers or suburbanites, you live alone or work long hours and have kids who don't come home right after school, this doesn't necessarily mean that you should forgo dog ownership. But it does mean you might have to arrange for someone to care for your dog during the day if your dog cannot tolerate isolation, at least for the first several weeks or months. A dog left alone for long hours is far more likely to become bored and unhappy; the dog is also more likely to develop destructive behavior problems, such as chewing things he shouldn't or barking and disturbing the neighbors, a major concern for urban dog owners. And because the dog is confined to the house, he's going to be uncomfortable if he is not given the opportunity to relieve himself periodically. Busy dog owners must be willing to be flexible to accommodate the needs of their dogs. If you want a dog but are worried about your schedule, consult Chapter 6 on Dog Schedules, Sitters, and Kennels.

## Your House

Consider the size of your home, the layout, and its contents. If you live in an efficiency apartment, or if your home has small rooms adorned with glass figurines, a large, high-energy breed of dog is not for you, nor is a tall dog with a long tail — it would be like having a bull in a china shop. But if you're lucky enough to have a home with spacious rooms, a larger dog could do some romping without causing damage.

How is your home furnished? If you have a lived-in house with a carpet chosen to resist dirt and you don't mind having to wipe a spot off the wall now and then, then you won't need to worry if you select a dog that might track in some mud. But if you take pride in an immaculate home environment, don't choose a dog that sheds a lot or one of the short-nosed breeds famous for snorting and slobbering.

Do you have a lot of steps? Then your home might not be a good place for a dog with a long body, like the dachshund or the corgi, which is prone to disk problems and might have trouble getting around the house.

If you live in a high rise where it takes considerable elevator time to get down and outdoors, consider a dog that can be trained to go indoors permanently in a box or on paper. If you have an apartment below you, consider whether you have well-carpeted floors that will muffle the sounds of a very active medium or larger dog trotting around.

And finally, no matter where you live, be sure that dogs are permitted! There is a federal law that protects the rights of seniors and handicapped people to own pets if they live in federally assisted rental housing. But if you rent anywhere else, keeping a pet might be prohibited by something in your lease called a *no-pet clause*. Other buildings allow pets, but with restrictions. Check this out before you buy a dog. Obviously, if you have a no-pet clause in your lease, it would be ridiculous to get a dog and set yourself up for hassles with the landlord, eviction threats, or the legal costs of fighting the clause. Problems do arise, however, when an inconsistent landlord lets one tenant have a dog and denies another tenant that right. If you already have a dog and some kind of pet clause is causing you trouble, you can get more information on this subject from the Pet Food Institute in Washington, D.C. An address is provided in the back of the book.

## Your Neighborhood

Survey the area around your home. You may have a small backyard or a dog walk where you can exercise a dog and take him to relieve himself at any hour of the day or night. Your condominium's community lawn is not a good place to use — even if you scoop the stool, the dog will kill the grass with urine, which is sure to draw complaints from neighbors. If you have a park nearby, is it a safe place to go late at night? Even a large dog may not be a deterrent to a determined mugger. Talk to dog owners in your neighborhood — chances are they will have helpful tips about the best neighborhood hangouts for dogs and their owners. If you do not have a safe, nearby outdoor area, or if you don't like the idea of having to pick up dog stool outdoors, again consider a small dog trained to go inside permanently.

## Your Budget

Dogs do cost money to own. They must be fed, get their shots, be licensed, and get treatment from a veterinarian when they are ill. If you want to keep costs down, select a small dog that eats less food than a larger dog. Some dogs require professional grooming, but many dogs do not. Some breeds have associated and potentially costly physical problems, such as hip dysplasia. No matter how carefully you choose a dog, unexpected illness is a possibility, and you must be willing and able to foot the bills.

# Dog Traits and Personalities

If you have a particular type of dog breed in mind, study the history of the breed; it will give you clues to the kind of personality a dog is likely to have. For instance, toy dogs were bred primarily for companionship and are more likely to be content sitting in their owner's lap than larger dogs. Terriers were bred for controlling rodents; they are going to be lively dogs.

Working dogs may have been bred for guarding or perhaps for pulling sleds; generally, they make excellent family pets but they tend to be the larger, powerful breeds that need an owner able to handle their strength.

Sporting and field dogs were primarily bred for working with hunters in the fields and woods. You can be sure that this kind of dog will need lots of vigorous exercise. Within this group are dogs such as the English setter and the Chesapeake Bay retriever, who may need far more exercise than the average urban dog owner can provide. But also included in this group are the golden and Labrador retrievers; they need lots of exercise, too, but are generally better adapted to urban living.

Hound dogs, such as the basset hound and beagle, which are known for getting on well with children, were bred for use in hunting because of their ability to track with their noses. That tells you that these dogs are more likely to wander off if given the opportunity.

Some established dog breeds don't fit into any of these dog classes but have their own unique histories.

## How to Learn about Different Breeds

The chart that appears later in this chapter will give you some idea about the breeds that might best adapt to your lifestyle. If you have no specific kind of dog in mind and don't know much about the different kinds of dogs, try to attend some dog shows. Just remember that people who show dogs are going to be a lot more serious about training their pets than average owners, so don't make judgments about a kind of dog's behavior based on what you see at a dog show. You can, however, ask general questions about the breed, then supplement that information by reading one of the many fine breed books available in bookstores or the library. A book that has beautiful color pictures of all the dog breeds recognized in the United States and good descriptive information about each is *Harper's Illustrated Handbook of Dogs,* edited by Roger Caras.

More breed-specific information on dogs, such as those most likely to bark or to be especially active in the house, can be found in *The Perfect Puppy,* by Benjamin L. Hart, D.V.M, and Lynette A. Hart.

Once you have a specific breed in mind, learn more about that kind of dog by taking the time to visit a breeder or even an average owner of that kind of dog: veterinary offices, your local humane society, and dog training schools could probably put you in touch, and there are certain to be dog breed clubs in your area.

## The Small Dog

In an urban area, small dogs are almost always easier to care for than larger dogs. The very small ones can get most of their exercise in the house. Larger dogs need more space to move around and usually need supplemental outdoor exercise to remain in peak condition and to help prevent behavioral problems.

Choose a very small dog if you want a dog that can be trained to go inside the house on papers or in a patio box, because the stool will be small. Indoor training is also a good choice for the elderly or ill who have trouble getting outside or for busy urban people who must leave their dog at home (preferably with a companion animal) for longer periods of time. Large dogs produce greater quantities of urine; they also have much larger stools — sometimes several daily — which can be difficult to manage if you must clean up after your dog indoors or outside.

Smaller dogs generally have a longer life span than larger dogs; some may live a healthy 14 years or more compared to only 8 or 10 years for some of the much larger breeds. This is an important point to consider if you want a dog that is, under normal circumstances, likely to live throughout your son's or daughter's childhood.

Compared to large dogs, small dogs generally will do a lot less damage during the puppy chewing stage than larger dogs with bigger teeth and stronger jaws.

**AN INTERESTING TIDBIT**
Did you know that some of the toy breeds require only one-third of a cup of regular dry food daily, but that a 100-pound dog requires about 7½ cups?

Some apartment houses will allow small dogs but not large ones; if there's a chance you'll be moving, there's likely to be less resistance to a small dog. And if you will be traveling with your dog, a small canine is more likely to be allowed in your motel or hotel room than a large dog.

A disadvantage to very small dogs is that they are often delicate and are less likely to tolerate rough handling by small children. They are also more likely than most larger dogs to be yappers and barkers. Even if that doesn't bother you, it might bother your neighbors.

## The Larger Dog

Some people prefer a larger dog — which here means any dog that's not a toy or small dog — because of the size alone; they like a dog they can really grab and bear-hug. Others simply think the larger breeds are more physically attractive.

A larger dog is less likely to get underfoot than a tiny dog racing around your legs, and is less likely to be a yapper than a tiny dog. They may be better able to hold urine longer than small dogs. And they are a better choice for very athletic people; most larger dogs can withstand lot more exercise than small dogs.

For the urban dweller worried about crime, a larger dog is certain to be more of a deterrent than a small dog.

Many larger breeds are like gentle giants — they are big but have calm personalities and may be more tolerant of small children than the smaller breeds. Then again, there are larger breeds not known for being good with children, ones that can be aggressive and need an especially patient but firm owner.

Generally it is said that, if you are willing to give your dog lots of exercise, you can have any size dog, even if you live in an apartment or row house. This advice can lead to trouble, though, because many average owners grossly underestimate exercise requirements. For some of the larger breeds, particularly the sporting and field dogs, one hour of vigorous, outdoor activity won't come close to satisfying their needs, and few urban people have time to provide two or more hours each day. If you've got your heart set on a large dog but have limited time to provide exercise, carefully consider the history and characteristics of the breed, or consider an older dog of that breed.

## The Dog Coat

There's more to a dog's coat than short or long; some dogs require more grooming than others because of the type of coat they have. If you're a busy person already worried about meeting the needs of a dog, don't complicate matters by getting a dog with a coat that requires extensive grooming.

Short-haired dogs generally leave less hair around the house to clean up than long-haired breeds, but there are exceptions. If you aren't overly concerned about shedding and select a dog that leaves hair around, there are cleaning aids to help keep your house free of dog hair.

Consider the smell of the dog's coat, since urban owners live in close contact with their dogs. Some dogs have no odor at all; others have coats with a characteristic smell that some people love and others abhor. Some dogs don't smell until they get wet, but then they can fill the house with an odor that you might detest.

## Consider the Climate

If you're a winter walker or if the temperatures dip low where you live and you want to walk your dog a few blocks away to let her relieve herself, do not select a delicate, short-haired dog that is going to be cold even if you put a coat on her. Generally these are toy dogs, but some of the larger dogs, such as the whippet, will not tolerate cold, rainy, windy weather. Likewise, if you have swelteringly hot weather in your area, do not select a dog unable to tolerate heat unless you have an air-conditioned home and can safely exercise the dog during the cooler early morning and evening hours. Breeds to avoid in this case might be the pug and some of the other short-nosed breeds. Even a dog that can generally tolerate hot weather might get her paws burned on that hot city pavement if you can't carry her.

## Always a Pup?

The major advantage to getting a puppy is that you train the dog yourself the way you want him trained. Puppies usually are weaned and ready to go home at about eight weeks of age.

In contrast, adult dogs may have already developed behavior problems, which may be one reason why previous owners got rid of them. However, for busy people who have limited time to train a puppy or who don't want a lively puppy racing around the house, an older dog might be a wiser choice if you can get reliable information about the dog's background.

If you have children, be sure you obtain firsthand information if you opt for an older dog: Don't take someone's word that an older pet is "great with kids."

## How Many Dogs?

If your dog is going to be left alone for more than several hours daily, consider getting two small dogs or a dog and a cat. Two puppies or a puppy and kitten raised together are going to get along better than two older animals that have been strangers, though it might be possible to find a family with two congenial adult pets that need a new home. Another possible source for finding two compatible dogs might be breed rescue clubs in your area; one of the club members might be keeping two dogs awaiting placement that have already demonstrated compatibility.

Considering how much trouble one isolated dog can be, two animals that can be trained to go on paper or in a box in the house might save you trouble in the long run. Two animals are less likely to become lonely and generally will exercise each other playing.

You'll hear from some trainers and breeders that if you have two dogs they will become dependent on each other, form their own pack, be less affectionate with the owner, and more likely to act aggressively. However, there are many average dog owners with a happy family of humans and multiple dogs. If your animals are happier because they have companionship, then you're going to be happier in the long run, too.

## A Male or Female Dog?

For urban dog owners who want to train a dog to use an indoor bathroom, a male dog that hikes his leg to urinate is obviously a poor choice — get a female. Female dogs of some breeds are considered easier to train. They do come into "heat," which can be an unpleasant event, but if you are like most average owners and have no interest in breeding your dog, you should have the dog spayed.

If you are interested in a larger dog and are concerned about exercise requirements, the females of some breeds are somewhat more docile than the males.

If you have fallen in love with a male dog, it's a dog you will be taking outside anyway, and it's a dog of a breed not associated with aggressive tendencies, then by all means that's the dog you should have.

## How to Use the Following Owner Profile Charts

The charts are designed to give you ideas about the kinds of dogs that would suit your lifestyle; just select the owner profile that most closely matches your own, then read on. All the dogs in the charts were selected because they are likely to do well in an urban or suburban area with the owner profile described. Here's a rundown on some of the categories:

"Easy to groom" means that only minimal to moderate brushing and an occasional bath are required to keep the dog's coat in good shape.

"More likely to do well with kids" means just that — but keep in mind that even dogs known for getting on well with children will snap or bite if they are abused or teased. On the other hand, almost all dogs, even the tiny toy breeds, will do well with family children who are old enough and well behaved enough to treat a dog kindly and gently.

"Watch for overbreeding" means that these dogs are so popular that some breeders breed them en masse, with little regard for temperament. If you are interested in one of these breeds, be especially careful to find a highly recommended, reputable breeder specializing in family pets.

The exercise definition given in each chart is intended for dogs in their prime — puppies, elderly dogs, and ill dogs of course would require less exercise than is advised here. Exercise needs vary greatly among dogs; two dogs of the same breed can have different energy levels. But the definition should help keep you from underestimating those needs, in which case you could end up with a dog that chews, barks, and generally drives you nuts. You'll learn more about determining exercise needs in Chapter 9.

The comment section provides additional breed-specific information. All of the breeds in the charts have their own wonderful characteristics, but information you might consider a negative is also provided.

## Potentially Difficult Dogs

Because dogs living in a densely populated area will be exposed to a lot of people and to other dogs, their owners have a particular responsibility to select a dog they can handle — and certainly one that's unlikely to act aggressively.

Listed below are a few of the breeds that have been associated with aggressive behavior. If these dogs are well bred and properly trained, they almost always make wonderful pets. But poor breeding, especially coupled with the wrong training or no training at all, could result in trouble. If you are interested in one of these breeds, be sure to get your dog only from a highly recommended breeder and only if you are willing to get professional dog training.

**German Shepherd** — These dogs need careful socialization and training. They are guard dogs and may get into trouble unnecessarily defending their owners. They are also shedders.

**Chow Chow** — An especially appealing puppy that looks like a cuddly ball of fur, this dog can grow into a ferocious adult. Incidents of biting humans and other dogs are thought to be the result of owner ignorance about the dog's temperament and need for firm handling. Chow chows also need considerable grooming.

**Pit Bull** — This term really applies to the American Staffordshire terrier but is used loosely to include the Staffordshire bull terrier and the bull terrier. They have been associated with deadly attacks on humans. The reason? Poor breeding and irresponsible owners who intentionally train dogs bred specifically to fight in a way that fosters their aggressive tendencies. There has been a movement to outlaw pit bulls in some areas. The anatomy of these dogs makes their bite powerful and damaging.

**Doberman Pinscher** — A dog overbred as it came into popularity several years ago, this dog, like the pit bull, has fallen victim to irresponsible breeders and owners who foster aggressive tendencies. Breeding is thought to have improved recently.

**Rottweiler** — Again, as popularity has increased, so have incidents associated with the breed, including a deadly attack on a human. This is a dog for a more experienced dog owner or an owner committed to getting professional training.

# Where to Get a Dog

Before you buy a dog, think about this: There is an explosive population of dogs that breed "wild," die from starvation, disease, or accidents, or are picked up by the dog catcher to be put to sleep at the animal shelter if not adopted or claimed. The problem is so bad that some dog advocates believe dog breeding should be greatly limited and that pet stores should not sell dogs — only pet supplies — so that more dogs will be adopted from the animal shelters. Since selling dogs is a money-making business, such limitations would be hard to impose, but we can each make a contribution to controlling the pet population problem by considering a dog from the animal shelter and by having our dogs neutered or spayed.

## The Animal Shelter Dog

The major advantage of getting a dog from your local animal shelter is the cost, which is next to nothing. You'll also be saving the life of a dog that would be put to sleep if not claimed or adopted. And, through the humane society and cooperating veterinarians, dog owners also are often able to get a discount on neutering or spaying their dogs.

Most dogs at the shelter are mixed breeds; about 40 percent are purebreds. If you make a careful selection, you are just as likely to have a lovable pet as the owner who paid a huge price for a purebred. But there are drawbacks. You usually can't find out much about the dog's background. If you are looking for a puppy, there is no way to tell exactly how large the dog will grow unless the predominating breed is obvious.

There are lots of adult dogs at the shelter that ended up there either because their owners didn't like their behavior or because they got lost, wandered far from home, and did not have an identification tag. Some are left there because their owners simply didn't want to make an effort to care for their dog — it's heartless, true, but at least they didn't dump the dog on a street corner and drive off, which happens a lot more frequently than you might think.

THE GUILT-FREE DOG OWNER'S GUIDE

## Owner Profile 1

You are not home all day or cannot get outdoors much when you are home. You want a small female dog (or two) that can be permanently trained to go indoors on paper or in a box, and one that can get most of her exercise in the house.

| Breed | Approximate Weight Range | Type of Coat |
|---|---|---|
| Affenpinscher | 6–9 lbs | Wiry; doesn't shed |
| Bichon Frise | 7–12 lbs | Fluffy |
| Chihuahua | 2–6 lbs | Smooth or long |
| Chin, Japanese (also called Japanese Spaniel) | 4–7 lbs | Long |
| Dachshund, Miniature | 10 lbs | Smooth, long, or wiry |
| Maltese | 4–7 lbs | Long |
| Papillon | 8–10 lbs | Somewhat long |
| Poodle, Toy | 4–8 lbs | Curly; doesn't shed |
| Shih Tzu | 7–18 lbs | Very long |
| Spaniel, English Toy | 9–12 lbs | Somewhat long |

THE DOG CHOICE

**Exercise definition:** Daily indoor play sessions and occasional outdoor walks or trips when possible for socialization; any of these dogs, however, would enjoy daily walks when you are able to provide them, and all, of course, could be trained to go outdoors to relieve themselves.

| Easy to Groom | Good with Kids | Comments |
|---|---|---|
| Yes | | An adaptable dog with a comical, monkey-like appearance. |
| | Yes | Lively and affectionate; watch for overbreeding; some professional grooming needed. |
| Yes | | Active dog that can be aggressive toward strangers and children, but can be an ideal lap dog for an adult. Some are notorious yappers. |
| Yes | Yes | Affectionate dog for owner who would enjoy lavishing attention; regular brushing needed; sheds. |
| Yes | Yes | Humorous, playful dog; not good for homes with many steps because of its long back; watch for overbreeding. |
| | | Needs lots of grooming unless you keep its coat clipped short; may not tolerate small children, but its adorable appearance and adaptable nature make it an ideal dog for urban adults or families with older children. |
| Yes | | Likes lots of attention; hardier and more tolerant of weather changes than other toy dogs. |
| | | Highly intelligent; likes lots of attention; some professional grooming needed; some are yappers. |
| | Yes | Very affectionate and is more tolerant of children than other toy dogs; lots of brushing needed. |
| | Yes | For owners who enjoy grooming; ears and eyes need regular attention. |

## Owner Profile 2

You have no backyard, nor do you want to have to take a dog outside to soil early in the morning and late at night. You want a small female dog trained to go indoors on paper or in a box permanently. You would, however, want to take the dog for regular outdoor walks.

| Breed | Approximate Weight Range | Type of Coat |
|---|---|---|
| Greyhound, Italian | 6–15 lbs | Short, smooth |
| Griffon, Brussels | 8–12 lbs | Smooth |
| Pinscher, Miniature | 9–10 lbs | Smooth |
| Poodle, Miniature | 10–16 lbs | Curly; doesn't shed |
| Schnauzer, Miniature | 14–15 lbs | Wiry |
| Terrier, Cairn | 14 lbs | Shaggy |
| Terrier, Toy Fox | 3–7 lbs | Short, smooth |
| Terrier, Toy Manchester | 6–12 lbs | Short, smooth |
| Terrier, Norfolk | 10–12 lbs | Wiry |
| Terrier, Norwich | 10–12 lbs | Wiry |

THE DOG CHOICE

**Exercise definition:** Daily indoor play sessions; in addition, outdoor walks five or six times a week for about 10 to 20 minutes each, or divided into two shorter walks daily. Any of these dogs, however, would enjoy longer walks if you can provide them, and all could be housebroken.

| Easy to Groom | Good with Kids | Comments |
|---|---|---|
| Yes | | Mild-mannered; needs firm but gentle owner, since this dog's feelings are easily hurt; not tolerant of cold weather and doesn't like being left alone; sheds little. |
| Yes | Yes | Lively and needs lots of affection; intelligent, but can be stubborn about training. |
| Yes | Yes | Adaptable but active; can be noisy; barely sheds. May get into mischief if left alone. |
| | | Needs lots of attention; easy to train; needs some professional grooming; watch for overbreeding. |
| Yes | | Lively, personable dog; can get into mischief if left alone too much; some are yappers. Some professional grooming may be needed. |
| Yes | | Energetic, adaptable dog, but some are yappers. |
| Yes | | Lively; easy to train, although some are barkers; hardy, but not a cold-weather dog. |
| Yes | | Affectionate and easy to care for but, like all terriers, a lively dog. |
| Yes | Yes | Known for adaptability; especially friendly dog. |
| Yes | Yes | Like the Norfolk Terrier, a very adaptable dog; slightly different appearance from the Norfolk. |

THE GUILT-FREE DOG OWNER'S GUIDE

## Owner Profile 3

The dog can go outside to soil — either you have a yard to use or you are willing to take the dog out when he has to go, even if it's early on a winter morning — but you want a dog that still requires minimal to moderate amounts of exercise.

| Breed | Approximate Weight Range | Type of Coat |
|---|---|---|
| Basenji | 21–24 lbs | Short, smooth |
| Beagle | 18–20 lbs | Short, smooth |
| Bulldog | 40–55 lbs | Short, smooth |
| Corgi, Cardigan Welsh | 20–40 lbs | Somewhat long |
| Dachshund, Standard | 17–25 lbs | Short, long, or wiry |
| Hound, Basset | 50–60 lbs | Short, smooth |
| Poodle, Standard | 50–55 lbs | Curly; doesn't shed |
| Sheepdog, Shetland (Sheltie) | 20 lbs | Very long |
| Spaniel, Cocker | 25–28 lbs | Very long |
| Terrier, Boston | Under 15 lbs to 25 lbs | Short, smooth |

THE DOG CHOICE

**Exercise definition:** Walks five or six days a week ranging from about 15 to 30 minutes each, or divided into two daily walks. Daily indoor play sessions. Any of these dogs would enjoy and benefit from longer excursions, except for the bulldog.

| Easy to Groom | Good with Kids | Comments |
| --- | --- | --- |
| Yes | | Very playful, clean dog; described as catlike by owners. Doesn't bark, but can vocalize loudly and can get into mischief if left alone. Best for people with previous dog experience. |
| Yes | Yes | Pleasant personality; watch for over-breeding. Some are barkers or stubborn about training. |
| Yes | Yes | For owners who want a relatively inactive dog; needs walks to keep weight down; cannot tolerate hot weather or overexertion. |
| Yes | | Likes lots of attention. Not good for homes with lots of steps because of the long back. |
| Yes | Yes | Humorous dog; some hard to train. Like Corgi, has a long back and not good for homes with many steps. |
| Yes | Yes | Easygoing , but can be stubborn about training. Ears may need special care to keep them free from odor. Long back, so shouldn't have to go up and down stairs a lot. |
| | | Usually easy to train and house-break; watch for overbreeding; professional grooming needed. |
| | Yes | Easy to train; loyal. Some bark; don't like strangers; shed. |
| | Yes | Especially sweet and affectionate dog, but watch for overbreeding. |
| Yes | Yes | Small variety can be house-trained; can't tolerate hot weather or over-exertion. |

THE GUILT-FREE DOG OWNER'S GUIDE

## Owner Profile 4

The dog can go outside to soil — either you have a yard to use or you are willing to take the dog out when he has to go no matter what the time or the weather. You are an active family or individual, able to give the dog maximum outdoor activity.

| Breed | Approximate Weight Range | Type of Coat |
|---|---|---|
| Boxer | 60–75 lbs | Short, smooth |
| Collie, Bearded | 50–75 lbs | Long, thick |
| Dalmation | 50–65 lbs | Short, smooth |
| Dane, Great | 100–150 lbs | Short, smooth |
| Retriever, Golden | 55–75 lbs | Moderately long |
| Retriever, Labrador | 55–75 lbs | Thick |
| Schnauzer, Standard | 30–50 lbs | Wiry |
| Terrier, Airedale | 45–55 lbs | Wiry |
| Terrier, Irish | 25–27 lbs | Wiry |
| Whippet | 20–28 lbs | Short, smooth |

THE DOG CHOICE

**Exercise definition:** Five or six days weekly, brisk walks from 20 to 90 minutes, depending on dog's energy level, or two shorter walks. Walks should be supplemented with runs in an open fenced-in area whenever possible, with the activity determined by your dog's level of fitness. On days you can't get the dog outside, there should be lots of indoor play activity.

| Easy to Groom | Good with Kids | Comments |
| --- | --- | --- |
| Yes | Yes | Energetic dog; wonderful companion; can be destructive when left alone. Light shedder; drools; intolerant of very hot weather. |
| | Yes | Playful; easily trained; needs lots of brushing. |
| Yes | | So energetic that may be destructive when left alone. Heavy shedder; watch for overbreeding. |
| Yes | Yes | A gentle giant that's relatively inactive indoors, but needs long outdoor walks; short life span; costly to feed. Some have congenital heart and bone problems. |
| Yes | Yes | Easy to train and loves children; watch for overbreeding! |
| Yes | Yes | Easy to train; adaptable. |
| | Yes | Thrives on human companionship; don't leave alone a lot. May need professional grooming and obedience training. |
| | Yes | Playful and fiesty; for the firm owner interested in obedience training. |
| | Yes | Loyal, but needs firm handling; may be aggressive toward other dogs. |
| Yes | | Gentle, sweet dog; easy to train; doesn't like cold or rainy weather. |

## The Breeder's Dog

The major advantage of buying a dog from a breeder is that you can find out about your dog's background and, in some cases, get documents verifying that a particular line of dogs is free of conditions, if any, that affect certain breeds. Breeders generally sell puppies, and you can observe the dog's parents to get an idea how your dog is likely to look and act when fully grown.

If you use a professional breeder, be sure that you go to a reputable one recommended by knowledgeable friends, by the local humane society, by other dog-advocate organizations, or by a veterinarian. Assuming the reason you want a dog is for family companionship, the breeder should be concerned with producing good family pets for average owners, not the animal's physical traits for show. Be wary of anyone who seems mainly concerned with unloading puppies for profit.

There are also amateur breeders, such as the neighbor whose dog has been bred. In this case, the dogs may not have been selectively bred for temperament as the professional breeder's dog would have been. Then again, the puppies might be the product of two wonderful dogs. You can still find out more about the dog's background than you would if you went to an animal shelter, and the dog is probably going to cost you less than the professional breeder's dog.

The best breeders will extensively question prospective dog owners about their lifestyles and living situations; they may even insist on seeing your home and evaluating its readiness for pets. If you are truly concerned with what is best for both you and the dog, you should welcome such inquiries.

The cost of buying a dog from a professional breeder is far more than you would pay at the animal shelter and varies widely depending on the breed; $200 to $300 is not unusual for some of the more common breeds. A breeder, however, is likely to be cheaper than pet stores in urban areas.

## The Pet Store Dog

The major selling point of pet stores is convenience; a pet store has dogs of many types where you can see them all in one place. Pet store owners claim that their dogs are more sociable because they have been exposed to employees, customers, and browsers.

In recent years, however, some pet stores have been widely criticized for inhumane treatment of animals. For instance, employees in a Virginia pet store — part of a national pet store chain — staged a walkout, alleging that the owners let sick animals die because it was cheaper than getting proper medical care for them. The humane society investigators reportedly found a small dog with a highly infectious disease and a retriever with muscle atrophy from being kept in a cage so small that moving around was impossible.

Dogs in pet stores are often purchased from the puppy mills, where breeders produce dogs in mass quantity for profit, often in filthy conditions, and with little or no regard for breeding dogs of good temperament. And how many pet store owners have you heard of who carefully question a prospective owner about his or her lifestyle and living situation?

If you want a pet store dog, be sure that the store has a reputation for providing humane care for its animals and for selling healthy dogs. If you buy a dog from a pet store with a bad reputation, you are only supporting the inhumane treatment of dogs.

## The Final Choice

You're a step away from selecting your dog. You've considered the kind of dog you want and where to buy the dog; now consider the dog's individual personality and physical condition.

### Checking a Dog's Personality

Since urban owners especially need to select a dog that will be good around other people, carefully observe the dog's temperament. The dog should be alert and friendly. You and your family should gently pet, handle, and talk to the dog before buying to observe the response to your physical and vocal gestures; dogs with a good temperament obviously will welcome the interaction and will gladly come to you.

If you are buying a puppy, a widely recommended method of testing temperament is to cradle the dog in your arms as you would a baby, with the dog's stomach up, and to tip the dog's head back a bit. A puppy with a calm temperament should settle down comfortably in your arms and not struggle violently to get away. A dog that becomes paralyzed with fear during this maneuver might be a particularly shy dog. This could be a dog that has trouble adjusting to the noise and congestion of a crowded area without special conditioning.

Do not buy a dog that tucks her tail between her legs and slinks or paces around or one that generally seems nervous.

### Physical Check

Examine the dog methodically, from head to tail, to make sure the eyes are clear, the ears are clean, and the gums pink and healthy. Is the dog's coat shiny and clean?

If you're looking at a puppy, check the tummy for protrusions, which could signal a hernia, or for a bloated look, which could indicate worms.

Check the dog's stance to see that the legs look properly aligned, and make sure that the dog doesn't limp or walk awkwardly.

Check the dog's vision by seeing if he reacts to your movements, and the dog's hearing by seeing if he reacts to your voice or clapping.

If you find a problem in a dog you've got your heart set on, consider whether the problem can be treated. Ear mites, for instance, are a common ailment that can be eliminated with proper therapy from a veterinarian. If you have any doubt at all about a dog's medical condition, request that a veterinarian check the dog out before you buy.

If you are buying a purebred dog, the seller should have registration papers for you to complete and send to the American Kennel Club.

Many places that sell dogs allow for a veterinary examination within ten days of purchase, and if a major problem is found, a full refund is given. Ask about this policy before you buy!

## Checklist for Prospective Dog Owners

The following list will help you review important points to consider before finalizing your purchase. You should be able to answer "yes" to every question or statement or have a viable alternative solution.

_____ Companionship is the primary reason we want a dog.

_____ Does everyone in the house want a dog?

_____ Are dogs permitted where we live?

_____ Will we keep the dog if our living or family situation changes in the future?

_____ Is there one reliable person in the household who wants the primary responsibility of caring for the dog?

_____ Will our family schedule permit us to meet the needs of the dog for attention and exercise, or will we be able to make special arrangements to accommodate those needs?

_____ Is our home large enough to accommodate the dog, and, if not, are we willing to provide enough outdoor activity to meet the dog's need for space and exercise?

_____ Is the dog's temperament likely to be compatible with our family lifestyle?

_____ If the dog is of a larger breed, can we handle him or are we going to devote considerable time to training him?

\_\_\_\_\_ We have considered the dog's potential for shedding as well as the suitability of the dog's coat for our climate and are confident there will be no significant problems.

\_\_\_\_\_ We can meet the dog's grooming needs.

\_\_\_\_\_ Our neighborhood has a convenient place we can take the dog to relieve herself, or we have a yard or can train the dog to use paper or a box indoors.

\_\_\_\_\_ We know the dog's expected life span.

\_\_\_\_\_ We can afford a dog.

\_\_\_\_\_ We feel satisfied that the dog is coming from a reputable source.

\_\_\_\_\_ We feel confident the dog is healthy, or we are willing to see that the dog gets any necessary treatment.

\_\_\_\_\_ We have considered the sex of the dog.

\_\_\_\_\_ We are certain that we want a dog and that, once obtained, the dog is here to stay.

\_\_\_\_\_ We can't wait to get the dog home!

## You Made a Poor Choice

Let's say that, for whatever reason, you acted on impulse and you have a dog not exactly compatible with your lifestyle. The most important thing to do is to make a decision quickly about whether or not to keep the dog.

### When You Can't Keep the Dog

If, unfortunately, you realize that you are not going to be able to meet the dog's needs or that you simply do not want to take on the responsibility of caring for the dog, then the kindest thing you can do is to immediately take steps to find the dog a better home; the longer you keep the dog, the harder it will be for the dog to adjust to a new home.

If you got the dog from a breeder, perhaps the breeder will take back the dog. You might not be able to get your money back, but consider it a lesson in life. If that's not an option, do everything you can to keep the dog happy and healthy while you search for a home. If necessary, hire a pet sitter to help.

Your local humane society can put you in touch with organizations that find owners. Put up notices in veterinary offices, post signs at grocery stores, run an ad in the newspaper, and spread the word fast among friends and relatives. When you find any prospective owners, check them out carefully yourself, taking care not to let them make the same mistakes you made! Conduct a home visit to see if the people live in a way that would indicate the dog will have a good home. If they are good potential owners, they should welcome this request. Do they want a dog as a family companion? Do they have time to spend with the dog? Use the checklist above to help determine their suitability as dog owners.

Be especially careful about checking out prospective owners you get from running newspaper ads. Phyllis Wright, vice-president for companion animals at the Humane Society of the United States, says that some of the people who respond to these ads are those who buy dogs to sell to laboratories for experimentation. They may go to great lengths to falsely represent themselves — some may show up with a child in tow to make it appear that they want the dog as a family pet. Get references on prospective buyers!

If you cannot take proper care of the dog while you find him a new home, then he may be better off at a shelter, although he could very well be put to sleep if unclaimed or not adopted in a few days.

## You Want to Keep the Dog

If you want to keep the dog but clearly have a mismatch on your hands, there are numerous ways to handle the situation; many are outlined earlier in this chapter. If you are not home all day, the dog is chewing wildly, and the neighbors are complaining about the howling, then you've got a dog that cannot tolerate being left alone. You may need to find dog day care, at least until the dog adjusts and until you are able to do some training. *If you really want to do it, you can solve virtually any problem you have that relates to your dog.* The other chapters in this book will tell you how to deal with problems of schedules, dog sitting, and problem behavior.

If you have both the compassion to understand your dog's needs and the motivation to use a systematic, common-sense approach to dog care, the payoff is huge: many years of loving companionship.

## The Best Answers to "A Quiz for Prospective Dog Owners"

1) **c.** Willingness to help a lost dog shows compassion and decency toward animals. An answer of "b" is the next best; there's the risk that a dog left at the shelter could be put to sleep if not wearing an identification tag and if not claimed, but taking a lost animal to the shelter is better than leaving him out loose to be hit by a car.

2) **a.** This answer shows you keep the value of material possessions in perspective — an important trait for dog owners. An answer of "c" is good, too — most dog owners should not have white carpeting!

3) **b.** A dog is for keeps! Most pet problems can be solved if the owner uses the right approach. If you answered "c," it means you are unnecessarily leaving yourself open for a lot of aggravation and that you are establishing a poor relationship with your pet.

4) **a and b.** Most happy dog owners have a good sense of humor; one of the delights of having a dog is watching their antics. They realize that, especially during the puppy stage and until a dog is trained, anything in their home is "fair game."

5) **b.** This question is based on a true story! The correct answer here is an indication that you understand that a dog should not be punished for doing what you taught him to do. An answer of "c" — correcting the dog — is okay if you caught the dog in the act.

# CHAPTER 2

# THE NEW DOG IN THE HOUSE

*The First Few Days*

T hink about the sounds of an urban area. There are fire and police sirens, honking horns, cars backfiring, road crews with drills, neighbors banging, music playing, and a lot of strange people walking around. Keep in mind that a dog's hearing is a highly developed sense that enables her to hear sounds we cannot. In an urban area, the dog's ears are going to tell her there's a lot going on. Couple all this with the trauma of a strange new home and new owners, and you can begin to understand how frightened a new dog in the house can feel.

## When to Bring the Dog Home

Some dogs will settle right in — you can bring them home one day, go to work the next day, and the dog won't make a fuss. That's unusual, though. Most dogs, especially puppies, need several days or weeks to adjust and to feel secure; bringing them home and then promptly leaving them alone in strange surroundings is not the way to help them adjust. If everyone in your family works outside of the home on weekdays, the best time to bring a dog home is during a holiday week. The next best is a long three-day holiday weekend, followed by a regular two-day weekend. Do the best you can. If your work schedule is a problem, see Chapter 6 on Dog Schedules, Sitters, and Kennels.

Dedicating yourself to these first few days will save you problems in the long run; a dog that has been given a chance to adjust is less likely to start barking, whining, and chewing up the house. And you're likely to find that any "trouble" the dog causes is far outweighed by the fun of nurturing and observing this latest addition to your family.

This is also the time to have your dog licensed and to arrange for a trip to the veterinarian, where the dog can be checked out and given any necessary shots. The veterinarian may advise that puppies not be taken outside until they have had all the shots necessary to prevent them from contracting infectious diseases.

## First Impressions

If you are driving a puppy home, keep him in a padded box; speak soothingly to the dog and pet him. Avoid driving the dog home during rush hour, and make the ride as smooth as possible.

Bring the dog into the house calmly, without a lot of fanfare, maintaining the soothing, friendly voice. If you have a puppy, put the dog into her space (see below) and stay with her for about 15 to 30 minutes before you go to other areas of the house. Come back frequently to check on the dog so she knows she hasn't been abandoned.

If neighbors make a loud racket or a loud siren goes off outside, don't make a big deal about it so that the dog won't either. Use a soothing voice to tell the dog "It's okay," then go about your business; you're giving the dog the message that these are everyday, acceptable occurrences.

An older dog might want to walk around and investigate; if he's housebroken, that's what you should let him do. If there are a lot of other family members in the house, ask them not to all converge on the dog at once; let the dog seek them out, and each family member should give a friendly, gentle greeting as the dog approaches.

Whether you have a puppy or adult dog, keep groups of non-family members away for a few days if you sense the dog is even the least bit apprehensive about his new environment.

For puppies, play sessions should be gentle and short; too much exercise can be harmful to them because their bodies are not yet fully developed. Reading Chapter 4 on dog safety is an absolute must for any dog owner, especially if you have a puppy in the house, and so is Chapter 5, The Polite Dog, where you will learn about selecting a proper collar and leash for your dog.

## Other Animals in the House

Your major goal is to keep your current pet — dog or cat — from feeling threatened by the new dog. Let the animals get to know each other at their own pace, and be sure to give the animal already in residence lots of attention so that he or she associates the newcomer with something positive. Cats are territorial creatures, and it may take a while for them to adjust to a new dog.

## Your Dog's Space

Puppies should have their own space, whether they are tiny toy dogs or large-breed puppies. It is virtually the unanimous opinion of dog experts that puppies are better off confined. It makes them feel secure, it keeps them safe, and it protects your home from puppy accidents and chewing.

THE GUILT-FREE DOG OWNER'S GUIDE

Dogs are considered puppies until they are about a year old, but, like humans, each dog matures physically and behaviorally at a different pace. Your dog may be using his special space for a long time, so make the effort to select and prepare it as soon as you have your dog, if not before.

For apartment and city dwellers, creating this special place can be difficult because space is usually tight anyway. You have several options; whichever you choose, just make sure that the dog's place is warm, but not hot, and is free from drafts. Also make sure the dog is confined in such a way that he can see out around him.

Do not lock your new dog — no matter what his size or age — into a closed, tiny space, like a bathroom with a solid door or a dark, dingy basement. Dogs don't like it any better than you would, and they are more likely to howl with misery, disturbing neighbors. Although dogs, especially puppies, like to feel secure, they don't like to be alone. Some are downright claustrophobic, unable to tolerate confinement in tiny spaces, and some are afraid of the dark.

Periodically, let the dog out of his space to explore, at his own pace. If he is hesitant to take a look around, don't push him.

Adult dogs that are housebroken and that are not chewers will probably be happier if left to roam the house, although you might want to confine them at first to one larger room or to one floor of the house, gradually increasing their freedom as you become confident that they will behave.

## Using a Room

A room is the ideal place to make a space for your dog. Since the dog is supposed to be a family companion, and since a companion should be able to live out and about the house, giving your dog a room is the first step in teaching your dog to behave in the house. The kitchen may be your best choice because it usually has floors that are easy to clean and little or no furniture that a dog can destroy. It's also well trafficked by the family, which is a plus, since your dog will want to be around his new "pack." If you have an open-style kitchen that can't be blocked off, create a space for your puppy in another area of the house where the dog will be secure but not too isolated.

**TIP**

The first few times you leave your dog alone in the house, do so only for a few minutes at a time a few times each day, so that she becomes confident that you'll return. And when you leave, do so matter-of-factly; remember, you don't want the dog to think this is a big deal.

THE NEW DOG IN THE HOUSE

Perhaps a corner of the family or living room can be used, even if you have to move some furniture around.

To confine the dog, use a baby gate to block the doorway. Be sure to choose a gate that the dog cannot chew pieces off of and one with holes small enough to ensure that the dog's head can't get caught in it. The gate should be high enough to discourage larger puppies from trying to jump over. You can buy gates made especially for puppies from pet supply stores and catalogs.

A bathroom might be a good place if the door faces out into other areas of the house — such as the kitchen or living room — and if you block it off with a puppy gate so the dog can see out.

## Indoor Kennels

If you have a home with open rooms that can't be blocked off and puppy-proofed easily, and if money isn't a big problem, a good option is an indoor exercise pen or kennel for your puppy. You can buy steel wire kennels already made with a dog's safety in mind. They create a room within a room for your dog. It's a great idea for renters who don't want to take a chance on a teething puppy destroying structural property like doors and baseboards, or for people particularly concerned about puppy accidents. The product list in the back of this book gives information on how to order an exercise pen and have it delivered to your door.

To give you an idea of what's available from one company, you can order eight panels, each 42 inches high and 24 inches wide, and with one panel made into a gate, for under $120. You can have it shipped directly to your home for under $10. This would give you an enclosure with ample space, even for a large-breed puppy.

In such a kennel, there's enough space for the dog's bed and food at one end, if necessary a place to relieve himself at the other, and room left to romp. There's usually even enough room for you to crawl in and play with the dog a bit, which will help the dog associate the kennel with something positive. If you are worried about how an exercise pen will look in your house, just think how much nicer it will look than chewed-up furniture and stained rugs!

You can order a floor mat for the kennel, put it in the kitchen and cover the floor with papers, or if it has to be put on a carpeted floor, you could set it on plywood covered with plastic, then newspaper.

Although you could use the kennel as your dog's permanent room, it ideally should be used only until the dog is housebroken or paper-trained and old enough to be left out in the house.

If you decide on an indoor kennel, be sure to ask for an exercise pen, not a crate or puppy pen, which are much smaller. The puppy pen, however, which measures about three feet square, might make a nice-sized enclosure for one of the tiny toy breeds. Like puppy gates, puppy pens also are available through catalogs that sell pet products and through some pet supply stores.

### Crates

Some trainers and breeders recommend a crate for puppies, which is also intended to be used as a housebreaking tool. If you are interested in crating your dog, see the section on crating in the next chapter. Crating is a somewhat controversial topic, so if you want to use this option you should be well informed.

### Dog Beds

You can buy beds, but considering how much puppies like to chew, a cardboard box is probably a better choice; it's unlikely to hurt the dog if swallowed, unlike wicker beds, which can break into sharp, dangerous little pieces. A cardboard box is also light and can be moved from the puppy's space to your bedroom at night if you choose. Make sure the box doesn't have any staples in it!

The front of the box can be cut out so the dog can get in and out easily. Line the box with a clean blanket folded thick enough to prevent the puppy from being chilled by the floor. Use blankets without strings, edging, or filling that the dog can get caught up in or eat. And use old blankets; some battering is inevitable.

If you do buy a bed for your new puppy, get one with a metal or heavy plastic frame that the dog can't chew. These usually come with a nice cushion, although dogs have been known to destroy them. You might want to use a worthless old blanket until you are certain the dog is not an avid chewer.

A lot of dog owners still put a ticking clock in their puppy's box, which is thought to replicate the mother dog's heart and comfort a puppy. You should give the dog a sturdy chew and some toys, after you've read Chapter 4 on dog safety.

For adult dogs, you might obtain a bed from the previous owners, which would be good to use if it is familiar and comforting to the dog.

## Where Should the Dog Sleep?

There are no one-night stands with a dog. Once you let your pet into your bed, it's hard to get him out. There are owners, though, who are so comforted by the presence of their dog in the bed that they can't sleep any other way. Read on and then select the sleeping arrangement best for you.

## Sleeping in the Owner's Bed

Some trainers believe that if you let your dog sleep in your bed, the dog will begin to view you more as a pal than as a master and be less likely to obey. Average owners, however, might find that there are more mundane reasons to forbid your dog from getting into your bed. For instance, how large will your dog grow to be? Even if you have a king-sized bed, you might find yourself fighting for space every night if you have a heavyweight canine that likes to cuddle.

If you take a tiny dog to bed, it's possible you could accidentally kick the dog out onto the floor or roll over on the dog and injure him.

Dogs can wreck a lovely bedspread, especially if they belong to one of the larger breeds that tend to snort and drool. This problem can be solved by having the dog sleep on his own throw placed over your bedspread.

There is the possibility of catching diseases from dogs. Such diseases are called *zoonoses*. One example is streptococcal infection, which has been associated with "strep" throat in humans. There is a type of worm that children can catch from dog feces. For average dog owners, however, who keep their dogs clean and have them checked regularly by a veterinarian, the risk of catching anything from a dog is pretty slim.

If you want to let the dog sleep in your bed or your child's bed, at least try to train the dog to sleep at the *foot* of the bed, in a corner unlikely to interfere with the owner's sleep and to prevent the transmission of any zoonoses.

## Sleeping in the Owner's Room

If you are certain you don't want the dog in bed with you, consider letting the dog sleep in her own bed in your room or a child's room.

In their dog training manual, *How to Be Your Dog's Best Friend*, the Monks of New Skete say that in over 400 cases of problem dogs they've studied, 80 percent slept outside of their owner's bedroom, including those that slept just outside the doorway. The monks point out that letting the dog sleep in your room provides a time for extended but undemanding contact between you and your pet that builds trust and confidence. This can be especially beneficial for busy people whose dogs are somewhat isolated all day — like the dog that's cooped up all day in the owner's home. This "sleep therapy" is also good for hyperactive dogs, the monks maintain.

On the other side of the coin are trainers who believe that, if you let your dog sleep in your room, she may become so dependent on being with you that it will become nearly impossible to ever leave her at a kennel or at the veterinarian's should you ever need to.

Consider whether your dog is going to have to adjust anyway to your being out at times other than overnight. If you end up with a dog you can't kennel, use a pet sitter instead. An attentive, kind companion who cares for your dog in the dog's own home is likely to keep your dog happy while you are away, and help protect your home from burglaries, a fear of all urban dwellers.

# Dogs That Whine and Wet in the Night

*Expect to have several nights of interrupted sleep.* Assuming that you have decided not to let the dog sleep in your bed, expect your new dog to whine, cry, and try to crawl out of his bed and into yours. He may get excited and have an accident or two. It's normal! It's amazing the number of new dog owners who get rid of an adorable new dog just because the dog demonstrated this behavior the first several nights. What did they expect?

You can help minimize this behavior by doing the following: Before bed, have a play session, give the dog water, let the dog relieve himself, then bed him down for the night.

A puppy particularly will wear your patience thin, but have sympathy. He's a baby lonely for his warm litter and his mother. If he's already got an alarm clock ticking away underneath him, try adding to his bed a chew, some safe toys, and a hot water bottle carefully placed under his blanket so he can't get burned. Pet and soothe the dog into a calm state while he's in his own bed, then go to bed yourself.

The older dog that keeps trying to hop into your bed should be taken back repeatedly to his own bed, petted, soothed, and left alone.

If nothing seems to be working and the dog — puppy or adult — makes such a racket that you are worried about the neighbors complaining, try pulling the dog's bed next to yours where you can pet him to sleep. Chances are he's going to keep trying to crawl into your bed; keep putting him back into his own. If it's just not working, try exercising the dog some more — exhaust him within safe limits, let him relieve himself, and try again to get him settled.

Eventually, as he begins to feel more secure, you should be able to gradually move the dog bed away from yours and to a more convenient place in the bedroom. If your plan is to eventually move the dog out of the bedroom, it will take longer and more gradual conditioning.

## Talking to Your Dog

If he or she doesn't already have one, you'll want to give your dog a name right away to facilitate communication. Just about any name will do, so long as it's short, easy to understand, and doesn't sound too much like any of the command words you'll be using. A name with two syllables might be easier for the dog to understand than a name with one syllable.

Use the dog's name every time you speak to her so that she learns her name quickly; always use her name in a friendly manner, so that the dog forms a positive association with her name.

The dog names listed on the following page demonstrate how creative average dog owners can be and how many of them name their dogs with words that reflect something about their own lives.

## What Dogs Understand

It is said that dogs do not actually understand our language, that they are responding to the tone of our voices and to tones used in association with other signals. For instance, if it's just before the dog's daily feeding time, you're in the kitchen, and you brightly say "Dinnertime!" the dog is likely to wag her tail and let you know she's ready to chow down. If you make the same statement another time of day in a deadpan tone of voice while you are walking down the street, the dog is likely to respond with a curious "What did you say?" look.

For the average owner, it's not that important *how* dogs understand, but that they *do* understand and respond to an amazing variety of words and phrases used in certain ways and in certain situations. In addition to the list of commands you deliberately teach your dog, such as "Sit," "Stay," and "Heel," you will find that much of your "vocabulary" with the dog develops

### A Sampling of Dog Names

| Dog's Name | History of Name |
| --- | --- |
| Callahan | A Doberman pinscher owned by a family of Irish descent. |
| Barnacle | A papillon owned by a family of boating enthusiasts that spends most pleasant summer days cruising the waters of the Chesapeake Bay. |
| Raoul | A Spanish professor's dog. |
| Bogie & Bacall | Two Afghan hounds owned by a couple of movie buffs. |
| Keno | A gambler's dog. |
| Mercedes & Audi | Dogs of a car enthusiast. |
| Dickens | A writer's dog. |
| Bloomie Dales | A mixed-breed dog that belongs to a woman named Dales who likes to shop. |
| Fugly | An English bulldog. |
| Loki | A dog named after a mythological god of mischief. |
| Cortes | Named after the Spanish explorer, a dog with a tendency to roam. |
| Iodine | An adopted homeless mutt with a coat the color of iodine. |

without your even realizing it as the dog becomes integrated into your daily life. Before you know it, the dog will be at the front door as soon as you say "The kids will be home soon."

Besides responding to you, each dog develops her own unique movements and vocalizations to communicate with you; this behavior will begin to develop the first day you have your dog, so remember to observe these signals and to begin interpreting them. They will amaze you!

# Puppy-Proofing Your Home

The first and foremost reason to puppy-proof your home is to ensure that your dog doesn't hurt himself. The other major reason, and the purpose of this section, is to keep you from being chewed out of house and home.

You might have heard that, if you teach your dog what to chew and what not to chew, and if you provide him with chews and toys of his own, your house won't be destroyed. This is worthwhile advice, but it doesn't always work. Modern dog owners, with their typically busy schedules, usually aren't with the dog enough to provide consistent training. And you could literally fill your house with toys and chews and still come home to find that the dog has munched his way through the leg on the table.

Chapter 5 of this book explains more about why dogs chew — basically because they are teething, bored, anxious, or a combination of these factors. Your goal while you have a new dog is to keep common puppy targets away from the dog instead of trying to keep the dog away from the targets. The philosophy behind this approach is that a dog who never learns to chew forbidden items, especially during the adjustment period and while he's teething, is less likely to chew them later in life; he'll be in the habit of chewing the things you want him to chew because that's all he's ever had to chew. Make it hard for your dog to get himself into trouble.

## Systematically Survey Your Puppy's Space

Don't make the mistake most new dog owners make: They wait until the dog has begun to destroy the house, then take steps to protect each item the dog has chewed from further destruction — one by one. Before they know it, the list of things the dog has ruined is as long as their arm.

Be one step ahead of your puppy. Make a systematic search of the dog's space; start at one end and work your way to the other. Item by item, remove or protect each puppy target — meaning virtually anything that doesn't belong to the dog. If you are certain the dog can't get out of her space, you can limit puppy-proofing to that room and do more proofing as the dog learns to behave and is given increased freedom in the house. The exceptions are electrical cords, poisonous plants, and other items that could be dangerous to your dog; these should be inaccessible throughout the house forever.

Be sure to leave your dog, especially puppies that are teething, several safe chews and a few sturdy toys. And, for a soothing, special treat for teething puppies with sore gums, try frozen baby carrots; so suggests Stephen C. Rafe, a behaviorist and author who specializes in canine behavior problems.

### Things Dogs Chew

Here's a partial list of items dogs have been known to chew (some dogs, in fact, are both chewers and diggers). As you can see, not much is sacred to a dog, and some puppy targets can prove highly dangerous to your pet.

- baseboards and molding around doors and windows
- the corners of steps — especially carpeted steps with foam padding underneath
- curtains
- throw rugs
- chair and table legs and chair cushions
- shoes
- pens, pencils, and crayons
- candles
- telephone and electrical cords
- notebooks
- books (and dogs always seem to chew the last chapter so you'll never know the ending)
- tubes and canisters of medicine
- floor tiles (digging and chewing)
- the interior of a Volkswagen (this was a boxer)
- metal doorknobs (a pit bull frightened by a thunderstorm)
- dog bed cushions
- pillows (dogs find gutting these great fun)
- their owner's mattress (chewing corners, digging the center)
- anything in the trash can
- plants, including poisonous varieties
- anything wicker

## Puppy-Proofing Aids

To protect items you can't remove or block off, buy a product at the pet supply store called Bitter Apple and generously apply; treat the legs of furniture, baseboards, and molding if necessary. If you are concerned that this product might harm your wood furniture, put it on a rag and tie that around the furniture legs. Apply it to the corners of wooden cabinets.

Protect the edge of steps by blocking them off with a piece of furniture that can't be destroyed, such as a metal folding chair or perhaps an old metal chest.

If this sounds like a lot of trouble, it isn't really. Now that you know what to do and how to do it, it should take less than a couple of hours, including the trip to the store to buy any products you need.

### Protecting Christmas Trees

Even a young dog that is housebroken and well behaved enough to have the run of the house may find the annual Christmas tree too tempting to ignore. How can you protect your tree and the dog? First, place the tree in a corner. This will allow you to block off the tree with chairs — or, for a tiny dog, with a coffee table turned on its side — when you are out of the house. To keep the dog from knocking the tree over, use some sturdy twine to secure the upper half of the tree to the wall behind the tree.

Use satin rather than glass Christmas balls in case your dog does get hold of one, and place valuable or small, delicate ornaments high on the tree, out of reach. Don't leave wrapped Christmas presents under the tree — if you want presents there, use empty, wrapped boxes.

An alternative approach is to get a smaller tree and set it up on a table out of the dog's reach.

# CHAPTER 3

# THE HOUSEBROKEN DOG

*Housebreaking, Paper-Training, and
Box-Training Your Puppy; Dog Accidents;
and Cleanup of Dog Waste in an Urban Area*

**H**ousebreaking means training your dog to go outdoors and not to go in the house. If you have a puppy and want to housebreak him right away, you need to be home most of the time to train him. Keep in mind that puppies must be taken outdoors frequently — every couple of hours — until they are from four to six months old, when they develop better bladder and bowel control. Your veterinarian must also give the dog the appropriate shots and give you the okay to take him outside.

Your situation may be that you want the dog to learn to go outdoors, but that you are a busy owner with a work schedule that prevents you from initiating training as soon as you get the dog. Maybe the dog hasn't yet had all his shots. Or maybe you got your puppy at a time when it's raining ice outdoors, which would only make a young dog associate housebreaking with something negative rather than positive. If this sounds like your situation, paper-train the dog in the house and later convert the dog to going outdoors. You could have a male or female dog if your puppy is only a few months old — males usually don't start hiking their legs until about four to six months of age or later. However, keep in mind that this two-step method requires special patience and persistence; you will be teaching your dog one way, then breaking that habit to teach him a new way.

If your problem is that taking the dog outdoors to relieve himself anytime in the future is difficult — you have no backyard and you are handicapped, elderly, or simply hate getting up early in the morning — then let's hope you are selecting a small female dog that you intend to train permanently indoors on paper or in a box.

Whichever method you choose, you will find that training your dog isn't difficult, as long as you follow these simple rules:

**1)** Plan ahead, and persistently follow the method you choose. More often than not, a healthy dog that is having trouble being housebroken has an owner who is not approaching the task in a well-organized, methodical manner.

**2)** Never scold harshly, hit the dog, or make a big deal about an accident or where and how your dog goes; it's only going to make the dog a nervous wreck about his bathroom behavior and can lead to far more problems than you'll ever have by teaching him primarily through positive reinforcement.

Cleanup of dog waste in an urban environment is a topic that dog owners must carefully consider, since animal control laws requiring prompt cleanup are increasingly in force throughout the nation's urban areas.

Cleanup can be managed without too much trouble if you feed your dog food that will produce a compact stool and if you have the right tools for cleanup in your particular situation.

## Housebreaking a Puppy —The One-Step Method

Remember that housebroken dogs are totally dependent upon their owners for going outside to get relief. To emphasize the importance of taking a dog out often, put yourself in your pet's position: How would it feel if you were absolutely forbidden to go to the bathroom unless someone else took you there? You'd hope that the person in charge would realize how uncomfortable you are when you have to go and would take you out often!

## Selecting a Place to Go Outdoors
## When You Have No Backyard

Training your dog to go in the same place is important for urban dog owners, because a dog taught that she can go anywhere out of the house will go at will in places where cleanup isn't easy. You may have no alternative but to use street curbs, but you'll be cleaning up after your dog each time she goes and worrying about oncoming traffic each time you take your dog outside to go. You may be lucky enough to find a place where you don't have to scoop feces; some apartments and condominiums have a designated "doggie walk" where you can take your dog, and some even provide cleanup. Urban owners also need to consider safety — you might have a wooded area nearby you could use, but will it be a safe place to go late at night?

If you have a place outside other than the curbs or dog walks to take the dog but will have to clean up after her, consider whether the ground is suitable for easy "scooping." Dog stool can be very difficult to remove from grass; if the stool is the least bit soft, there is always residue left that a neighbor could step in. Dog urine kills grass quickly, and neighbors who take pride in their parks and lawns will not appreciate the yellow patches. A better spot would be a mulched place or a place with loose, absorbent dirt that also will absorb urine.

## The Small Urban Backyard

If you live in a row house, town house, or ground-floor apartment with a small backyard, that's probably the best place to train the dog to go; you'll appreciate the arrangement on those cold winter mornings. If your yard is all grass, lift a section up in the most inconspicuous place and put down a section of finely shredded bark mulch, which will also help mask odor.

If your backyard is all concrete or brick, cleaning up dog stool is a breeze with a scooper, especially if you can hose down the patio. However, if the dog urinates there, too, he will wet his paws and track it into the house. Consider creating a mulched place for your dog to use in a flower bed or putting a sandbox in the corner of the patio.

## When and How to Take the Dog Out

*You must get the dog outside every time he is likely to go.* For puppies, that means after they awake in the morning, after naps, after eating or drinking, and after playing. This usually translates into every couple of hours during the day and evening. Also, take the dog out anytime you see him begin to sniff around, acting like he's looking for a place to go.

The first time your dog goes outside, praise him highly. Tell him "Good boy" (or "Good girl"), pat the dog, and act absolutely delighted over his accomplishment. Try to use the same door each time you go outside, and select a word or phrase that you want the dog to associate with elimination; use it each time you take the dog to his spot. Eventually, the dog will tell you when he has to go out, usually by standing next to the door, or will go on your verbal command once you have him outside.

The first few times out, don't clean up after your dog — or, if you aren't in your own yard, leave just a bit of stool if you can, so that the scent will encourage him to go there again. You can also purchase a commercial housebreaking aid, usually a liquid with a dropper, or use a bit of ammonia.

---

**TIP**
Block off or surround your dog's backyard bathroom with a lovely trellis covered with ivy or flowers. Your dog will appreciate the privacy, and his bathroom will be out of view when you entertain guests in your yard.

---

### How Long Should It Take for Housebreaking?

It is possible to teach a puppy to go outside in as little time as one day. This doesn't mean that on the second day the dog will tell you when she has to go out — it just means she won't go in the house if you continue to take her outside often. For most dogs, housebreaking takes several days or longer; different dogs learn at a different pace. Even when she's gotten the knack, remember that she still will have to go very often until she's from four to six months old. The exception is overnight: When a dog is sleeping, urine forms less quickly, and (hopefully) your puppy will be able to make it through the night.

## The Crating Method

Some trainers and breeders recommend crating dogs. A crate is another name for a dog cage, and it is intended primarily to be used as a house-breaking tool. Crates can be bought at pet supply stores or through catalogs, or they can be made if you have building skills. Most crates have only a place for the dog to sleep; some have one side for sleeping and the other for the dog to use as a bathroom when he can't wait for you to take him outside.

Crating takes advantage of the dog's natural instinct to soil away from where he sleeps. If he's in a cage with just enough room in which to sleep, chances are that he won't soil; he'll wait for you to come home and take him outside to go.

Few dog advocates object to the judicious use of crating — a crate used temporarily for only a few hours at a time, just until a dog is trained. Of con-

THE HOUSEBROKEN DOG

siderable controversy, however, is the excessive use of crating — some dogs are crated all day while their owners are at work, all night while their owners sleep, and just about any time the owner isn't interacting with the dog. They are crated not just when they are puppies, but for most of their lives.

## Arguments for and against Crating

Advocates of crating describe the crate as a cozy indoor retreat where a dog is going to feel safe and secure. They say that crating appeals to dogs, and, to back that position, they cite the *denning theory* (in the wild, the wolf, ancestor and cousin to the dog, lives in a den).

Crating advocates also argue — sometimes rightfully so — that crating saves dogs. Dogs that wet in the house and chew the furniture would be dumped or destroyed by insensitive owners if the dogs weren't in a crate where they can't do damage. Crating in and of itself may cure behavior problems, advocates say, because it makes dogs feel secure. And since dogs sleep most of the time their owners aren't there interacting with them, the dogs might as well be in a crate.

Opponents of excessive crating cannot understand why anyone who wants a family pet would want a dog that is going to spend most of his life in a cage. Properly handled and trained, most dogs can enjoy the run of the house and have the freedom to sleep in a different spot if they want, get a drink when they are thirsty, or just look out the window at the people going by. Isn't that a better life than being cooped up in a cage?

What is the real motivation behind the advocates of long-term crating? Could it be a conscious or unconscious desire to ensure that the dogs they breed or train are good models? After all, a dog who lives in a crate most of his life rarely has a chance to soil or chew. Just about any kind of breeding is going to make the dog look good and any kind of training "successful."

Some dogs truly do seem to like their crates; they use them without any encouragement at all from the owner. Other dogs use the crate only when put there by owners, and without protest. Does that mean they like it, or are these dogs just the more submissive ones that don't protest even if they are uncomfortable being crated?

And what about dogs that absolutely will not tolerate crating? Some will whine, howl, or chew and claw until they are bloody to get out. Why don't these dogs have a denning instinct? Other dogs, such as those from poorly run puppy mills and pet shops, were never taken out of their cages and were forced to soil there. These dogs will soil in a crate because their clean instincts have been destroyed.

Randall Lockwood, Ph.D., director of higher education programs for the Humane Society of the United States and an animal behaviorist, is one expert who thinks crating too often is used as an "easy way out" by people who don't want to take the time to train and socialize their dogs. He believes crating is a method that has great potential for abuse. It makes far more sense to teach the dog how to live out and about in the house — which can begin with confinement in one room — from the first day you have the dog, even if you end up with some chewed-up shoes and an accident in the house.

According to Dr. Lockwood, crating is best reserved for use in special situations: perhaps temporarily for a dog with particularly troublesome housebreaking and chewing problems, until training efforts begin to take hold; or for a dog that is being badgered by small children and may find the crate a great escape.

And Dr. Lockwood, who has extensively studied wolves in the wild, points out that wolves only live in a den for the first six to eight weeks of life. That certainly brings into question the denning theory as an explanation for why dogs should be crated. Even if wolves subsequently use a den for sleeping, it is not forced containment, nor are they denied the opportunity to relieve themselves.

In their book *Understanding Your Pet*, experienced dog trainers Warren Eckstein and Fay Eckstein call crating the "wrong environment" for a family pet. Having to open the crate to interact with the dog interferes with the socialization process. Crated dogs can have emotional problems later on, and the Ecksteins say they've seen dogs that have really created havoc in the house when they were let out of the crate because they never learned how to behave in the house.

Perhaps most disturbing about the crating controversy is the force with which some crating advocates insist upon this method. People who object to crating are told they "don't understand dogs." That's an easy argument to make, since the dogs can't speak up for themselves. The message here is that if you are a dog owner who has been encouraged to crate your dog but you aren't comfortable with the idea, *don't do it.* It's your dog, and it's up to you to decide how best to train him. Don't be intimidated by the adamant breeder or trainer who tells you that you are ignorant about dogs — you might have a lot to learn, but no one is going to know what's best for your dog better than you.

## How to Use a Crate Properly

If you decide to use crating as an aid to housebreaking, that's fine; just use it judiciously. First make sure the crate is a safe steel one without nails or wire that could injure the dog, and that the dog isn't in the crate with a collar, leash, or anything else she could strangle herself with. Dogs that are crated and seem to like their crate probably will be happier using it as their overnight bed, too, although some dogs use a crate during the day and sleep in a bed in their owner's room overnight.

THE HOUSEBROKEN DOG

The crate should have enough room for the dog to stand up, turn around, and lie down in. There should be a padded floor — not wire, which is harmful to paws — covered with a thick, safe quilt or blanket, since the dog is going to be sleeping most of the time she's in the crate.

## Gradually Introduce Your Dog to the Crate

Don't just shove your dog into the crate and lock the door. First put safe chews and toys in the crate, encourage the dog to go in on his own, then give him a treat. Some trainers advise putting a piece of your clothing and chews that you've rubbed your hands on in the crate; your scent will make the items more appealing and comforting. As the dog becomes accustomed to the crate — which could take several days — begin closing the door. Leave the dog inside for only a few minutes the first few times. When you reach the point at which you feel the dog is comfortable, you can start going out while the dog is crated, only for a few minutes the first several times, with the time gradually increased.

## Feeding, Housebreaking, and Socializing the Crated Dog

Since puppies need to eat three to four times daily, depending on their age, and they must have plenty of water, you must be home or have someone else there at appropriate times to take the dog out of the crate, feed him, give him water, let him stretch his legs, and take the time he'll need to relieve himself before putting him back in the crate. That means every two to three hours. Overnight, when urine forms more slowly, puppies can probably go somewhere between five and seven hours if they have been sleeping. Use the same methods for taking the dog outside that are outlined earlier in this chapter. If your dog has been in the kind of crate with paper on one side, you should train him to use paper outdoors.

Some trainers do not think crated dogs should have water in their crates because it will make them have to urinate, and they will be miserable if they have to go and can't. But, since water is so important, and because you should be taking the dog out every few hours anyway, it's probably best to leave a small supply of water in the crate — in a bowl that can't be turned over — in case the dog gets thirsty.

Most of the time you are home, your dog should not be in the crate; he is with you, learning how to behave in the house and becoming socialized. Do not use the crate for punishment; you want the dog to view the crate as a positive, pleasant place to be if she is to be happy while in the crate.

As the dog matures and forms the habit of going outside, theoretically she should never go in the house. Because she is out of the crate and supervised and trained by you when you are home, she becomes socialized and learns to behave in the house. You gradually increase her freedom — start by leaving her confined in the kitchen for a very short time to see if she behaves. Eventually, she should not need the crate. However, you might want to leave the crate in the house for the dog to use as her permanent bed, even though you never lock the door.

## Long-Term Crating

If for some reason you want to leave a dog locked in a crate while you are away at work all day, it is true that some dogs seem capable of comfortably holding their urine for many hours. The dog must be old enough to have good bladder control — not a small puppy — and there's no real reason to use this approach except as a last-resort option. Perhaps your dog is wetting and chewing despite heroic training efforts and confirmation from a veterinarian that there are no physical problems contributing to the dog's behavior. Certainly, crating is better than getting rid of a dog, assuming that the dog is generally a well-treated and loved family member.

Dr. Joseph J. Seneczko emphasizes that, if you decide you must crate your dog for longer than a few hours at a time, the limit should be seven or eight hours. And dogs that cannot hold out that long should not be expected to. The dogs most likely to be able to hold urine for longer periods of time are big dogs. A problem here is that the larger dogs seem to like crating the least. The small dogs that do seem to like crating can't hold out as long because their bladders are small, says Dr. Seneczko, who, by the way, prefers confining dogs to a room rather than a crate.

How can you tell if your dog will be comfortable crated all day? If your dog goes every few hours when you are home and can barely make it six hours without going overnight, chances are he's going to be uncomfortable crated all day. Males generally have to go more often than females. You may have to have someone come in to take the dog outside if you can't.

And finally, if your dog turns out to be one that cannot tolerate crating — one that whines, howls, and frantically claws to get out despite your best efforts to accustom the dog to the crate — *absolutely do not crate;* a dog so traumatized cannot possibly develop into a happy, well-behaved family pet. Another approach, such as a pet sitter, should be used.

Dr. Lockwood proposes that, if you use a crate, you rent a video camera and film your dog for a day or two while you are out to see how he's doing. Is the dog sleeping peacefully, or is he whining and pacing in misery, perhaps because he has to relieve himself or because he cannot tolerate confinement in such a tiny space?

---

**TIP**
If you paper-train your dog, don't leave newspapers lying around the house in places you don't want the dog to go — like on the furniture!

# Indoor Dog Bathrooms

If you are going to be training your dog to go permanently in the house, you can select either newspaper or a box. Both are cheap and easy to use; just read on and select the method that you think you'll be happiest with. Remember that you must have a female dog to make this option work!

## Using Newspaper

If you are not going to be home most of the time to supervise your dog and you are going to be using newspaper, cover the entire floor of the puppy space, whether it be the kitchen floor or the floor of the dog's exercise pen. If your dog is very small, you might only need very thick newspaper to prevent urine from soaking through to the floor; if you have a larger puppy, you may need to put a plastic liner under the newspaper.

When the dog has to go, she'll probably select a place away from her food and bed. Praise the dog for using the paper, and use the word you've selected that you want your dog to associate with elimination. Clean up after the dog, but save one urine-scented piece of newspaper and, if you can stand it, a tiny piece of stool, to attract the dog back to the same spot.

Let the dog out of her space to explore the house after she eliminates if she wants to go; she will begin to associate good behavior with increased freedom.

THE GUILT-FREE DOG OWNER'S GUIDE

In a couple of days, remove some of the newspaper from around the edge of the room, so that the area the dog has to eliminate on becomes smaller. If the dog goofs and goes on the floor while you are there, very gently point her head toward the spot, tell her "No, no" firmly but not harshly, and put the dog on the newspaper to show her where she was supposed to go. You want to correct the dog, but not make too big a deal about her bathroom behavior. You may have to do this several times, but she'll eventually catch on.

Appreciate your dog's effort to go on the newspaper even if she isn't always successful. Occasionally, a puppy will hunch up, with feet precariously perched on the paper and rear end hanging over the edge; a stool hits the bare floor. Don't scold; praise her while pointing to the closest section of newspaper. She is a baby, without full coordination, and will outgrow this miscalculation.

Keep reducing the area of newspaper every couple of days, until there is only a small section left where the dog can go. In a short time, you will have only a small section of paper to clean up. If she uses the floor a few times in a row, take a step backward and increase the size of the papered area again.

If you are going to be home with your puppy most of the time and youwant her to go someplace other than in her puppy space, such as a bathroom, porch, or storage room, you will have to take her to that place frequently — just as if you were taking her outside — and praise her when she goes. As soon as your dog begins to get the knack, let her walk herself to her bathroom, although she still might need some guidance from you.

### Using a Box

Some dog owners train their dogs to go in a box, like cats. You'll want to buy the plastic type of box made for cats, which is available at pet supply stores, through catalogs, and at most grocery stores. You could put a box in the bathroom, in a storage room, or on a small patio or porch. For tiny pup-

---

**TIP**

If you want to use cat litter, use this tip from cat owners. Instead of buying plastic liners made especially for the boxes, it's cheaper to use trash bags. Insert the entire box inside a large trash bag. Put a newspaper in the box to keep the dog from tearing the bag open, pour litter on top of the newspaper, then fasten the open end of the bag shut with a rubber band. To clean the pan, simply turn the bag inside out, tie, and toss.

pies that cannot get over the edge of a plastic box, start out with a cardboard box with the front cut out.

The box can be filled with thick layers of newspaper; stool is picked up with a tissue or scooper and flushed, and newspaper with urine is discarded each time the dog goes.

Another option is to put litter in the box, which you might want to do if the box will sit on a porch or patio. The disadvantages of litter are that it costs money, compared to newspapers which probably you have around anyway, and that dogs might kick litter out of the box and track some of it into the house. Litter also has to be changed and can be heavy and messy when it's wet. However, litter is far more absorbent than newspaper, and the dog is less likely to get urine on her paws; with newspaper, she might wet her paws and get newsprint on them. You'll have to scoop the stool from the litter each time your dog goes, but you could let the dog use it several times for urination. In contrast, newspaper usually has to be tossed every time the dog urinates.

To train your dog to use a box, it's best to start the dog out with paper on the floor of her puppy space as described above. When you have your dog going on only one small section of paper, start placing the paper in a box. Since putting the dog's paper in a box might throw her off, you should do this when you'll be home for a couple days to guide the dog.

## Converting Your Dog from One Bathroom to Another

Converting your dog from going in one place to going in another should be initiated soon after you get the dog if at all possible. The longer the dog has been going in one place, the longer it's going to take to convert him, and it takes different dogs longer to catch on than others. Begin with an attitude of patience and persistence.

Convert the dog at a time when you will be home for at least two days and preferably three. If you will be converting from indoor newspapers to going outside, do it on a day when the weather is pleasant — cold is okay, but ice and hail are not.

Put a piece of newspaper your dog has soiled or his box with dirty newspaper at the new place you want him to go, whether it be somewhere outdoors or another place in the house. Put the dog on a leash in the house and keep him with you at all times so he can't wander off and go in his usual indoor spot. Keep taking the dog to the new place at the appropriate times — after waking, eating, drinking, and playing — and repeat the word you have selected for your dog to associate with elimination. Stay with the dog at the new spot for as long as possible. If you are outside, run him around a bit,

THE GUILT-FREE DOG OWNER'S GUIDE

which usually makes dogs have to go. Eventually, your dog will do what you want him to, and hopefully you'll be in the new place when he does. Give the dog a lot of praise!

Keep the dog on the leash with you in the house until he's used his new bathroom several times. After he's been successful for a couple of days, stop using the leash in the house. Leave the dog in his space for an hour or two without any newspaper to see if he waits to go, and take him to the new place often. If he does wait, praise him highly as you take him to the new place. If he goes in his old place, don't scold — clean up the mess and then backtrack: Put him on the leash, keep him with you, and work on taking him to the new place. Make sure you are taking the dog outdoors frequently enough.

Some dog owners take their dogs out but let them continue to use paper in their space when they aren't home. You will have to determine if your dog can adapt to this dual method — many dogs can — or if it's just going to confuse him.

Whatever you do, remember that dogs vary widely in their ability to catch on. Some dogs can be converted in a day or two, while others take longer. If you are patient and consistent and use positive reinforcement, it's hard to go wrong.

# Accidents

All puppies, and occasionally older dogs, have accidents in the house. Don't let anyone make you think otherwise. Few owners have the time that professional trainers do to spend with their dogs to speed up the house-breaking process. Experienced but average dog owners take puppy accidents in stride — they clean up the mess and forget about it, but forge on with training. And what a dog leaves on your floor or carpet can't be any dirtier than what we track in on our shoes — it's just messier.

*Cause for concern is the housebroken or paper-trained dog that breaks training* more than once or twice in a short period of time.

## Why Accidents Happen

The reasons dogs have accidents vary. Puppies get overly excited during play sessions and go, or they simply forget to wait until they are in the proper place to go. If your dog has been severely scolded and punished, he could be urinating out of nervousness.

Perhaps there is company in the house or other changes in the dog's environment that may have upset him. Has a key household member changed schedules? Maybe you have been unusually busy or preoccupied and unable to spend as much time as you usually do with the dog. If the dog

THE HOUSEBROKEN DOG

left you an accident in front of the door, chances are that he asked to go out but that you inadvertently ignored the dog. (This author's dog had two accidents in the house while this book was being written.)

If there are no obvious behavioral explanations, consider physical reasons. A dog being treated with steroid medication urinates more frequently and may even wet in his sleep. He can't help it. A dog who has had a vigorous play session, then drinks a lot of water before bedtime, may not be able to hold urine all night.

Urinary tract infections are not uncommon, especially in older dogs. They are characterized by increased frequency of urination, lack of control, and sometimes straining on urination. In older dogs, a break in training can signal diabetes. If a dog leaves a stool in the house and the stool is loose, the dog obviously has some kind of physical problem, though it may just be a temporary gastrointestinal upset.

## What to Do

A trip to the veterinarian is in order for any trained dog that has more than one accident in a short period of time. If there's a physical explanation, chances are there is a treatment.

In the meantime, if you are there when the dog has an accident, a neutral position probably is best — don't scold, but on the other hand don't do anything to let the dog think it's okay, which could confuse her.

If you think the dog's accident was behavioral in origin and you are there to catch her in the act, a firm "No, no" and a quick trip to the proper place will suffice. If you aren't there to catch her, scolding isn't likely to do any good — again a neutral position is best. Then try to correct the behavioral problem. If there are changes in the household upsetting the dog, try to keep the dog's routine as unchanged as possible. The dog wetting only when you go out may have developed a case of separation anxiety. See Chapter 5 for a remedy. Talk with the veterinarian about how to change the dog's diet and water intake in a way that won't harm the dog but that might help reduce the problem. Are none of these suggestions working? Then try completely retraining the dog as outlined earlier in this chapter, just as if the dog were a puppy.

If you have truly tried every possible remedy (that means giving each ample time to work) and consulted with your veterinarian, but the problem keeps happening, you may have to confine the dog. Unfortunately, some elderly dogs lose control; in this case, have mercy. Keep the dog in the kitchen or an indoor exercise pen with the floor covered with papers when you aren't there to watch the dog. Let the dog live out his life with his beloved family, and tough it out. Confinement certainly is a better option than traumatizing the dog by getting rid of him.

# Cleanup of Dog Waste Indoors

Here's all you really need to clean up most dog accidents: lots of paper towels, white vinegar, any kind of household detergent or liquid dishwashing detergent, and carpet cleaner with pet deodorizers.

### Dog Urine

For dog urine, white vinegar is the most effective and the least expensive product to use. It neutralizes the odor, which is important; if the urine scent remains, your dog will be encouraged to go in the same spot again. Regular household cleaning products generally do not neutralize dog urine odor; in fact, those that contain ammonia are not recommended because, to a dog, they smell something like urine. Vinegar is safe for use on most floors and carpets. If you are out of vinegar, try club soda, another cleanup favorite among dog owners.

Urine accidents should be cleaned immediately; the longer urine remains, the harder it is to get the odor out. For carpeting, first soak up the excess urine, spray or sprinkle with vinegar or vinegar diluted with water, and soak up the remaining moisture with fresh paper towels. If you want to further clean the spot, follow with a weak solution of liquid dishwashing detergent and water or a commercial carpet cleaner.

Urine on the floor should be wiped up with paper towels and cleaned with a detergent.

Urine-soaked newspapers and paper towels can be discarded with your regular trash if they are in a plastic bag, which should be sealed to contain odor. Puppy urine, however, has a very weak smell.

Keep white vinegar handy for quick cleanups in a small spray bottle for even distribution on carpeting.

### Dog Feces

Dog stool is usually easy to pick up and is best disposed of in the toilet. Tiny dogs have tiny stools that can be picked up with a tissue and flushed. If you are using litter in a box, you can buy a scooper, available for a couple of dollars at just about any grocery or pet supply store, to scoop and carry the stool to the toilet. Regular cleaning and use of a disinfectant in your toilet (not the continuous-cleaning kind, which could kill your dog if he drinks it), should prevent any health hazards. Keep in mind that cat owners have been flushing cat stools down their toilets for years.

If flushing the dog's stool isn't something you want to do, or if your dog's stool is large, you can wrap the dog stool in newspaper, double-bag it, seal the bags well, and put the bags in the trash or in an incinerator. However, in many urban areas, it is a violation of sanitation law to dispose of any kind of feces in the regular trash. Ask other dog owners in your area what they do to dispose of dog stool.

If your dog has diarrhea, get most of it up with pieces of cardboard or wads of paper towel; you may not have any choice other than to put it in the trash. Be sure to wrap it very well so it can't leak or its odor escape.

If the stool is on a hard floor, use a household detergent after wiping up. If the stool is on a carpet, use the commercial carpet cleaner with pet odor neutralizers. Some dog owners use vinegar for stool, too, before using the carpet cleaner to help eliminate odor.

If your dog's stool stained the carpet, which may happen if the dog ate food with dye in it, you're better off checking with professional carpet cleaners. You might have to have that section of carpet replaced or buy a throw rug to cover the spot.

# Cleanup of Dog Waste Outdoors

It's obvious that you can't really clean up dog urine, but you may have to deal with the odor if your dog goes in a small backyard near the house. In the summertime especially, the smell can be powerful.

If you can, regularly hose down the area. You can purchase a dog odor eliminator made for outdoor use from pet shops and pet supply catalogs; these usually are mixed with water and poured on the area; they contain enzymes that destroy the odor-causing bacteria in dog urine. They are expensive, around $12 for a 16-ounce bottle.

If your dog has an accident in the hallway of your building, clean it up with vinegar as you would in the house; your neighbors will appreciate your efforts.

### Dog Feces

If you have to scoop up after your dog on the streets, in parks, or on your association's community property, you can buy a wide variety of scoopers. A cheaper alternative is to use a paper cup and paper towels: Scoop the stool into a cup, stuff with the towels, and dispose of it. You can also use plastic bags you have left over around the house.

In New York City, dog owners are allowed to dispose of dog feces in the Department of Sanitation litter baskets if the feces are in a container that doesn't leak. Since in some urban areas you are not permitted to put dog feces into a public trash can, you may have to carry the feces with you for disposal elsewhere — such as in your toilet.

Ask other area dog owners what they do. If a place to dispose of dog feces turns out to be a significant problem in your area, perhaps a group of dog owners could contact the local sanitation department to request that a special kind of box be provided for disposal — it's done that way in London. Your efforts to keep your neighborhood clean should be appreciated.

If your dog uses a small backyard, the methods of disposal are similar; either carry the stool into the house and flush it, or find out from other area dog owners what you can do with it. If there are woods near your home that aren't used by humans, you might be allowed to dispose of it there (using a scooper and leaving no paper litter behind), but ask the property owners first rather than risk getting slapped with a hefty fine for disobeying your local cleanup laws.

Odor in your small backyard can be minimized by hosing off concrete or by having your dog use an area with mulch that is replenished often. You might want to buy some lime, which is very cheap, and keep a pitcherful of it in the backyard. Sprinkling lime on the stool before cleaning it up helps dry up the stool, masks odor, and helps keep bugs away. Keep the lime in a place where it won't get wet and where your dog and children won't get into it; it could burn them.

Owners of small backyards also could invest in a Doggie Dooley, a piece of equipment you install in your backyard for disposal of dog feces. To use it, you dig a hole several feet deep. A bucket is then placed in the bottom of the hole, which you fill with an enzyme solution that breaks down dog stool. The stool is then supposed to be absorbed into the earth. This product comes with a lid to cover the hole. Some owners just dig a hole, use a cheap bucket they already have, buy enzymes separately, and cover the hole with a board or trash can lid. This method can be a wonderful convenience if you have absorbent dirt in your yard, but if you have earth that is primarily clay, it won't work — you'll just have a messy backup that attracts bugs. The other concern for urban owners, who usually have a lot of other people around, is that someone will fall into the hole.

## CHAPTER 4

# THE SAFE DOG

*Eliminating Hazards from Your Home;
Children and Dogs; Traveling with Dogs; and
General Pet Safety*

The major hazard to dogs in an urban area is traffic. Dogs that are allowed to run free or that get off their leashes are virtually certain to be seriously injured or killed by a car. Even dogs generally well trained and obedient off-leash will take off if startled or if they see something tempting enough come by. You can eliminate the threat of traffic by never letting your dog outside unless he is on one end of a leash and you are on the other, and by being especially careful to see that he does not get away from you.

Having your dog stolen is another possibility, so don't leave your dog tied up anywhere or leave him unattended in an unlocked car. With these threats out of the way, you can focus on other pet safety concerns.

## House Hazards

It's amazing the kind of trouble a dog can get himself into within the confines of his own home. Even if your dog is past the puppy stage, take the time to make your dog's environment safe.

### How to Keep Your Dog from Getting Out

Urban dog owners who live in buildings with maintenance people coming in from time to time run the risk of the dog being let out accidentally. Try to be there when workers come and, if you can't, ask them ahead of time to take special care not to let the dog out. Reinforce your message by leaving a note on the door.

Another very real risk in urban areas is that your dog could escape through windows and balconies or, worse, fall from them to his death. Even tiny dogs that you wouldn't think could get to a window can jump up on the ledge or jump to the ledge from a nearby chair or table. Large dogs have been known to crash through windows and glass doors.

Always keep lower windows shut and locked, or install locks on bottom windows that prevent them from being opened more than an inch or two. Don't count on window screens to keep your dog in, either. If you can get to them from the outside, install sturdy nails around the edges of screens to prevent the dog from pushing them out. Sliding doors, low windows, or windows that go to the floor are best covered with drapes or blocked off with a chair to discourage a dog from trying to crash through them.

73

THE GUILT-FREE DOG OWNER'S GUIDE

If you have a terrace or porch, the dog should not be permitted to use it without your supervision unless you are absolutely certain he can't escape, fall, or jump off. If you have the kind of balcony that has open banisters, wire could be installed to keep the dog from falling, but it's unsightly and might not be permitted where you live.

## Strangling

Never leave your dog leashed near the top of a stairway where she could fall off and strangle herself with her own collar. Also, don't leave the dog alone near banisters wide enough for her to get her head between them; she might turn her head, think she's trapped, panic, and strangle herself. If your dog is old enough and well trained enough to have the run of the house while you are out, and you are worried about steps, banisters, and landings, confine the dog to one level of the house and block off access to stairways and landings with chairs or a puppy gate when you go out.

 Make sure your dog's collar isn't so tight that it could damage her skin or choke her, and not so large that she could get it caught on something and strangle fighting to get away. You may want to use a break-away collar when your dog is home alone, which will break off if the dog gets hung up on something and begins to struggle.

Those rounded, stiff handles on department store shopping bags are another place your dog could get her head caught if she's tiny; keep these bags up and out of reach, along with plastic bags, which pose a suffocation hazard.

## Electrical Hazards and Fires

Make sure electrical cords are inaccessible to your dog; dogs will chew them and can electrocute themselves. Keep wet dog noses out of electric sockets you aren't using by installing the flat plastic plugs sold to protect children.

Fireplaces should have screens in front of them, and dogs should not be left alone with a fire going; don't assume your dog will have the good sense to stay away. Glass doors for the fireplace, which can be closed when you aren't there to supervise, are a good idea.

To help ensure that your pets get out in case of a fire when you aren't home, there are window and door stickers available to alert firefighters that you have animals in the house and how many. The stickers can usually be obtained through pet catalogs and in pet supply stores. You should also ask a trusted neighbor or two to alert rescue people about your pets if there's ever a fire when you are away from home, or ask them to keep a key and to get your pets out if the building has to be evacuated.

To prevent a fire from starting in your own home, don't leave appliances on when you are out, especially the clothes dryer, or use candles the dog could knock over. If you smoke, wet the cigarette butts in ashtrays before throwing them into the trash can.

---

**MISCELLANEOUS SAFETY TIPS**
- Watch that your dog doesn't get slammed in a door. It could be deadly if you have a small breed or a puppy.
- Teach everyone in the house how to pick up the dog properly; for very tiny dogs, place one hand under the tummy area and the other hand around the dog's chest. Larger dogs need one arm around the chest and another around the back legs. Watch that small children don't pick up the dog and drop him.
- If your dog walks through any foreign substance outdoors, whether it be motor oil, a pile of garbage, or feces from another dog, wash and dry his feet well as soon as you get home.
- Forbid your dog from running up and down stairways and from jumping on and off furniture; he could break a leg, and young dogs especially, with growing bones and joints, could seriously injure themselves.

---

## Poisoning

Poisoning can occur through ingestion, inhalation, or skin contact with chemicals. Prevent your dog from being poisoned by taking the same precautions around the house that you would with small children — store all potentially dangerous substances up and out of reach or in cabinets with safety locks. Depending on the poison and the degree of exposure, the symptoms can vary widely and might include drooling, twitching, intestinal upset, excitability, wheezing, general nervousness, seizures, respiratory failure, and even death. Dogs that are young, old, or sick are generally more susceptible to the adverse affects of poisons than healthy dogs in their prime.

### Household Chemicals, Repair Products, and Miscellaneous Items

Household cleaning products, including detergents, are among the agents that could be poisonous to your dog; besides keeping containers out of reach, avoid exposing your dog to them when you are using them.

THE GUILT-FREE DOG OWNER'S GUIDE

Don't let the dog close enough to inhale spray cleaners as you use them or let her walk across a floor still wet with cleaning chemicals.

Some continuous-cleaning toilet bowl products can kill your dog. Don't use them, and don't let your dog drink out of the toilet at home, so she won't drink out of toilets elsewhere.

Antifreeze really isn't a household product, but it's often kept in the house and can be deadly. It presents a special problem, because animals will voluntarily drink it if given a chance; it tastes sweet to them. Don't keep antifreeze or other car products such as oil or windshield wiper fluid in the house or, if you do, keep them in an especially safe place so that if they leak your dog can't get to them.

Lead can still be found in wall paint in old homes and in some other products, such as batteries. Keep your dog from licking or eating paint and anything else that might contain lead, and don't forget to put painting-related products, such as turpentine and kerosene, in a safe place.

### Insecticides, Pesticides, and Herbicides

Never spray your dog or his bed with chemicals—or with disinfectants or anything else for that matter — unless the product is specifically recommended for use on dogs. Even if a product is said to be safe, some owners feel it's best not to use any kind of chemical near their dog, since there's always the possibility of an unknown hazard.

Dr. Jeff Hall, veterinary toxicologist with the Department of Biosciences, College of Veterinary Medicine, University of Illinois, says that the number and type of poisoning cases in dogs exposed to chemicals such as insecticides, pesticides, and herbicides predictably change with the seasons.

In the fall, when the weather turns cold and mice and rats start trying to get into buildings for warmth, the number of dogs poisoned with rat and mouse bait increases. Even if you don't use these products, your neighbors might, so watch out for these poisons and the dead rodents killed with them.

In the spring and summer, there generally are more dogs with toxic reactions to insecticides and pesticides used inside the house. Pesticides include products used to eradicate fleas and ticks from your home and those you use to treat houseplants for bugs. There are also more reactions among dogs allowed in outdoor areas treated with herbicides. Generally, the problem occurs when a dog is allowed into a recently treated area. Some of the herbicides used can cause severe gastrointestinal problems, some cause kidney damage, and, in some animals, they can cause paralysis if the level of exposure is great enough.

Dr. Hall has some general recommendations for protecting your dog from the potentially adverse consequences of exposure to herbicides, pesticides, and insecticides:

**Indoors.** After treating your home with one of these products, including those for fleas and ticks, keep the dog off the premises for 24 hours. Carpets should be vacuumed, and any dusty residue on surfaces wiped away with a wet rag. Keep in mind that dogs will be walking and lying on the rug, rubbing up against furniture, and then licking themselves. They will be ingesting some of the product unless you clean it up.

**Outdoors.** If you live near an outdoor lawn treated with lawn-care products or if you have treated the flower beds in a small backyard with chemicals, again wait 24 hours before letting your dog into the area. If a spray has been used, begin counting to 24 hours from the time the spray has dried. If a granular product has been used, water it in and begin the countdown to 24 hours after it's dry, Dr. Hall advises.

**Treating your dog for fleas and ticks.** "At all times follow the label directions. However, if the directions are confusing, or if you are treating an animal less than one year of age, an old animal, or a sick animal, do so with great caution and watch the animal carefully for reactions," Dr. Hall advises. If you are using a flea spray on a young dog, for instance, spray a rag and then rub the dog in one small area rather than applying the spray directly to the animal. Then wait several hours to see if the dog appears to have any adverse reactions. Also, avoid overtreating your dog with a variety of flea and tick products. If you take your dog to the veterinarian for a flea dip or if you spray the dog for fleas yourself, don't then put a flea collar on the dog, too, without first asking your veterinarian about it, Dr. Hall says.

### Hazardous Foods and Food Poisoning

Dogs can get food poisoning from eating spoiled food or from food that is moldy. The symptoms might include vomiting and diarrhea and, in some cases, seizures. Give your dog only fresh food, and keep the trash can in a place where the dog can't get at it. Did you know that Valentine's Day, Christmas, and Halloween can be hazardous to your dog? The number of dogs poisoned with candy increases around these yearly celebrations, Dr. Hall says. The reason? There's more chocolate around, and, one way or another, the dogs get it. Chocolate is toxic to dogs because it contains caffeine and theobromine and because a dog's metabolism is different from a human's. Giving a dog a piece of candy can be comparable to a human drinking 10 to 15 cups of coffee in a very short time. And the smaller the dog, the less chocolate it takes to make the dog sick. Baking chocolate is by far the most potent and sweet candy the least; semisweet falls somewhere in between.

The first symptoms of chocolate poisoning usually are vomiting and diarrhea; hyperexcitability follows. Dr. Hall says that the owners of affected dogs invariably say, "I've never seen my dog act this way before; he's bouncing off the walls." If the dose is large enough, the symptoms get progressively worse; muscle tremors and even seizures can occur, and life-threatening abnormal heartbeats may develop.

It's essential that your dog get medical treatment quickly. But, of course, prevention is the best cure. Simply don't give your dog anything with chocolate in it.

### Plants

Many common household plants are toxic or poisonous to dogs. The effects can vary widely, ranging from a mild skin rash, which can occur just from contact with certain plants, to severe reactions including convulsions, respiratory failure, and death. More serious reactions are likely to occur with ingestion. Here are just some of the common houseplants that can be toxic to your dog:

| | |
|---|---|
| Aloe vera | English ivy |
| Amaryllis | German ivy |
| Azalea | Holly |
| Boston ivy | India rubber plant |
| Caladium | Jerusalem cherry |
| Calla lily | Mistletoe |
| Cineraria | Philodendron |
| Creeping fig *(Ficus pumila)* | Pothos |
| Daffodil | Potted chrysanthemum |
| Dieffenbachia (Dumb-cane) | Spider chrysanthemum |
| Elephant's-ear | Weeping fig *(Ficus benjamina)* |
| *(Caladium hortulanum)* | Yew |

The safest approach is to keep all plants up and out of reach of your dog, unless you know that the plants are nonpoisonous. Here are some common houseplants that are considered safe — as long as you haven't treated them with chemicals — according to the National Animal Poison Information Network:

| | |
|---|---|
| African violet | Japanese rubber plant |
| Baby rubber plant | Kalanchoe |
| Bamboo palm | Norfolk Island pine |
| Boston fern | Peperomia |

Coleus
Easter lily
Elephant's-ear begonia
   (*Begonia albo-coccinea*)
Gloxinia
Grape ivy
Hibiscus
Hoya
Jade plant

Prayer plant
Rex begonia
Schefflera
Spider plant
Swedish ivy
Variegated wandering Jew
Wandering Jew
Zebra plant

There are a variety of outdoor plants and shrubs, including the azalea, holly (including the berries), and some kinds of mushrooms, that could harm your dog if eaten. Remembering all the potentially dangerous ones is next to impossible, so the common-sense thing to do is to keep your dog away from all outdoor plants and shrubs.

## Toys

Toys are particularly important for indoor or confined dogs; because they are confined, they need as much encouragement as possible to exercise indoors, and playing with toys will help keep their interest and prevent boredom.

Toys must be carefully selected for each dog; a toy that's perfectly safe for one dog might put another dog at substantial risk for choking. Make sure that any toy you buy your dog is free of small parts and that the toy can't be torn apart into small parts that your dog could swallow. Always observe your dog with a new toy long enough to make sure the toy is going to hold up and that it is safe for your dog. With the exception of bones and chews, most toys are not going to be much fun for your dog unless you play with her.

## Bones and Chews

Rawhide is often recommended for dogs, but there are potential hazards. Rawhide pieces torn off and chewed can expand and swell in the stomach, causing gastrointestinal irritation and upset. It's also possible they could cause an intestinal blockage. Dr. Joseph J. Seneczko advises against rawhide bones, but, if you insist on buying them, he suggests that you avoid the chips or sticks variety and instead buy solid rawhide bones that are so large it's impossible for the dog to tear into pieces. American-made rawhide also is recommended over imported rawhide; questions have been raised over the years about chemicals used to treat imported rawhide.

A better choice for a bone or chew are some of the Nylabone products. They are made of nylon, and the bones cannot be chewed off in pieces. There are a variety of shapes and sizes. If your dog doesn't seem to be developing an interest in his Nylabone, try boiling it in beef or chicken broth. Or try rubbing your hands on it to make it more appealing. This company also makes a product called the Gummabone, which is made from somewhat softer material that your dog may find more appealing.

Don't give your dog food bones, particularly chicken and beef bones that can splinter; your dog could wind up with an internal puncture wound.

---

**TIP**

Most dogs enjoy carrying around a stuffed toy, but those bought at a store often have small parts — eyes, ears, and noses — that can be torn off and swallowed. Dogs will also eat the stuffing. If you have a sewing machine, try making your own safer stuffed toys. Cut heavy material such as canvas into a simple shape — a bone, perhaps — then stuff it with old socks and stitch it thoroughly, so that your dog cannot pull it apart easily. Take it away and make a new one if your dog tears or shreds the toy.

---

### Bells and Squeakers

Many commercial dog toys contain bells and squeakers that dogs enjoy, but most dogs can dislodge these noisemakers and swallow and choke on them. It's best not to buy them, but, if you do, let the dog play with them only when you are there to supervise and make sure that the toys stay in one piece. Put the toys away when you aren't there.

### Finding Toys That Last

Owners who find that their dogs destroy just about any toy they have should try latex toys, which hold up better than vinyl toys. Another sturdy toy is the Kong, made of rubber and manufactured by the Kong Company in Denver. It comes in different sizes and will withstand some serious abuse by dogs. It's available in some pet supply stores and through some pet catalogs. The King Kong, for larger dogs, costs from $12 to $15, but will hold up a lot longer than other toys. These are good outdoor toys; they bounce off the ground and go a different direction each time, which may help keep your dog's interest.

## Balls

Balls should be sturdy enough so that the dog can't chew them or pop them and eat the pieces; they should also be large enough so that the dog can't get them lodged in his throat. Even if a dog ball is labeled as being "for large dogs," use your own judgment to determine if it's a safe size for your dog.

## Pull Toys

Some trainers object to pull toys — toys designed to play tug-of-war with your dog. There's concern that it could encourage aggressive behavior or damage the dog's jaw. Yet it's a game many owners play with their dogs. If your dog is not of a breed associated with naturally aggressive tendencies, and if the dog has not demonstrated any potentially aggressive behavior, playing tug is probably okay if you don't pull too hard or long. Don't make it a war game. Buy a sturdy tug toy and, with puppies, hardly pull at all; their bones and joints are not yet formed, and you could injure them if you pull too hard.

# Seasonal Hazards

Dogs that live indoors in a controlled climate are going to be less tolerant of outdoor weather conditions than outdoor dogs with coats that grow thick in winter and that thin out in the summer.

## Heat

When you get too hot, you sweat. Dogs, however, don't. They cool themselves by rapid breathing, and it doesn't work as well. They are less tolerant of heat than humans. Dogs with short noses, such as pugs, boxers, and bulldogs, are particularly intolerant of hot weather because they don't breathe as efficiently as the long-nosed breeds. Dogs who become overheated could become dehydrated and suffer heatstroke. Dogs with light hair or body areas with no hair and with lightly pigmented noses can also get sunburned.

Avoid the hazards of hot weather by keeping your dog out of the hot sun and by taking care not to overexert your dog when the temperatures climb. Absolutely *never* leave your dog locked up in a car in hot or even warm weather; the car will get hotter than the outdoor temperature quickly, and the dog could die in a short time if his body temperature gets too high.

If you have a small backyard or terrace that you let your dog use, don't ever leave him there chained and without shade and lots of water.

If you don't have air-conditioning and it's hot, cool your home with fans, placed safely out of the dog's reach, and make sure your dog has lots of water to drink so he doesn't become dehydrated. If the indoor temperature becomes so hot it's unbearable for humans, you can bet it's too hot for your dog — take him with you to a friend's house with air-conditioning. If you can't do that, keep him cool by frequently patting him down with cool towels and by giving him lots of water to drink.

Urban owners need to remember that the hot city pavement or sidewalks might burn their dog's paws; walk your dog in the cooler morning and evening hours when appropriate.

## Cold

One of the most serious consequences of cold weather is *hypothermia,* a dangerous drop in body temperature that can lead to total collapse and death in a dog. Dogs that are puppies or that are tiny, such as the toy breeds, dogs with short coats, and elderly dogs are more susceptible to cold-weather hazards.

There are other hazards: Dogs can get frostbitten on their ears, their paws, and, in males, their scrotum. Icy sidewalks could cause your dog to slip, fall, and break a bone.

If you have a very delicate toy dog, especially one trained to go on newspapers or in a box indoors, don't take him out in freezing weather if you don't have to, unless you carry him and have a sweater on him. Some of the larger breeds that do not tolerate cold weather, especially cold, rainy, and windy weather, such as the whippet or the Boston terrier, also should have a coat or sweater on them if you take them outdoors; they should do their business and immediately come back into the house.

**TIP**

If you don't have a dog sweater on hand, or have a barrel-chested breed that is hard to fit with commercially made dog sweaters, try using a human sweatshirt — yours for large dogs and a child's for small dogs. The arms can be shortened with scissors, and if the waist is too large, gather some of the material and tie it with a rubber band.

If ice is a problem, prepare a clear, safe path for you and your dog before you take the dog outside to go, and if your dog has walked on streets or sidewalks where ice-melting chemicals have been used, including salt, wash and dry her paws when you get her inside.

## Children and Dogs

Children and dogs can be a wonderful combination, but kids are kids and dogs are animals, and all dog owners must keep in mind that there is the potential for dog bites.

Dog bites happen for different reasons. Small children who don't know any better pull the dog's ears, bang on the dog, pull the dog's tail, and hit the dog with toys. Older children with a mean streak can be deliberately cruel to dogs, hitting and teasing them. The dog bites to protect himself or as a warning. In some instances, dogs may bite for no apparent reason.

The most common type of bite wound in the United States is the dog bite; the annual incidence is an estimated one to two million, according to a 1987 article in *American Family Physician.* The authors also point out that a dog bite can be delivered with a force of 150 to 450 pounds per square inch, enough to do some serious damage to a child's face, leg, or arm.

Children are more likely than adults to be bitten by dogs, and stray dogs are not the usual culprit. Bites are more often inflicted by a dog that the children know — the neighbor's dog or the family pet.

Here's how you can help prevent dog bites:

- Never leave your dog alone with your own very young children, unless you are extremely confident that the dog is tolerant.

- Never ever leave your dog alone with young children who are not yours, and do not assume that, because the dog is tolerant of your children, he'll be tolerant of other children.

- Even if your dog is a breed known for being good with children, do not assume that he will tolerate children if he has not been raised with them. These dogs must be gradually conditioned to the presence of children.

- Teach all your children and visiting children to treat the dog with respect — in fact, demand it. Never let children — or adults, for that matter — tease, hit, or poke the dog, and do not let children scream and run around wildly in the presence of the dog. Explain that dogs

**DOG SAFETY CHECKLIST**

_____ Windows and screens in the house are secured.

_____ Patios or terraces are secured for dog safety or are inaccessible to the dog.

_____ Building maintenance people will not come into our home without notifying us first.

_____ There are no stairs, banisters, or landings in the dog's space that could present a hazard.

_____ The dog has a collar that fits properly.

_____ Electrical cords are out of reach.

_____ Household cleaning agents are inaccessible to the dog.

_____ Poisons, including insecticides and similar products, are inaccessible to the dog, and we know how to use these products without posing a hazard to our dog.

_____ Small items that are potentially dangerous, such as batteries, are out of reach.

_____ There are no continuous-cleaning agents in the toilet.

_____ Car products such as antifreeze and windshield wiper fluid are out of the house or out of reach.

_____ Home remodeling products such as paint and related materials are safely stored.

_____ Plants are safe or out of reach.

_____ Toys for the dog have been carefully selected for safety, and we have observed the dog with the toys to ensure that they cannot be torn up and swallowed; toys we aren't certain about are not given to the dog unless we are there to supervise.

_____ Bones and chews cannot be broken into small pieces and swallowed.

_____ Balls are not so small that they can lodge in the dog's throat.

THE SAFE DOG

are animals, not humans, and that they may bite because they are afraid the children will hurt them.

- Teach your children to stay away from strange dogs.

- If you've got a dog that's a snapper, see Chapter 5, The Polite Dog, and keep your dog away from other people. In an urban area, that can be difficult; strangers, including children, will want to come up and pet the dog. Do not hesitate to state nicely but firmly, "He's not used to children (or strangers); please don't come any closer." Avoid an unpleasant incident — and a potential lawsuit.

## Keeping Your Dog Safe on the Road

Many dogs love riding in the car. Riding helps to socialize them, and if you're a busy owner concerned about meeting the needs of your pet for companionship, it's one more opportunity to be with your dog.

Your dog may take to riding right away, but if she's a puppy or an apprehensive older dog, gradually introduce her. Start out with very short, quiet rides — don't go at rush hour. Act like you are having a great time and don't take the dog anyplace she might associate with something unpleasant.

If you have a sedan, have the dog sit or lie down in the back seat. Don't let her get into the habit of roaming around the car, since she's more likely to fall if you stop quickly. If you have a two-seater or a pickup truck, have the dog lie down next to you in the front passenger seat.

If you own a station wagon and have a larger dog, and you plan to take her on frequent car trips, con-

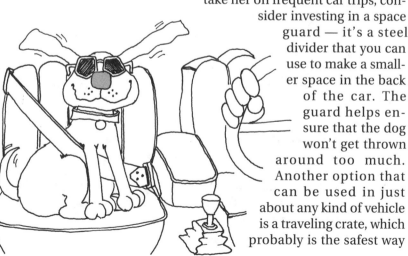

sider investing in a space guard — it's a steel divider that you can use to make a smaller space in the back of the car. The guard helps ensure that the dog won't get thrown around too much. Another option that can be used in just about any kind of vehicle is a traveling crate, which probably is the safest way

THE GUILT-FREE DOG OWNER'S GUIDE

to transport your dog.

If you have any kind of convertible, don't ride around with the top down when your dog is in the car so she won't be thrown out if you wreck.

There are dog car seats available from pet supply stores and through pet catalogs. One kind is a seat for small dogs; they are harnessed in but are up high enough to see out of the car. Another kind is a large harness for large dogs. Guy Hodge, director of data and information for the Humane Society of the United States, says that he is not aware of any safety testing on these devices, but overall he thinks they are a good idea. They prevent the animal from jumping around inside the car, which could distract the driver and cause a wreck, and they ensure that the dog can't jump out of the car. On impact, chances are they could keep your dog from being thrown and killed.

Here are some other rules of the road for dogs:

- This point was mentioned before in this chapter, but it is so important that it merits mentioning again. If the weather is the least bit hot, *do not leave your dog in the car.* Even if it's cool outside, be sure to leave the windows cracked so that he gets air. And only leave him if you can keep an eye on the car to ensure that he isn't stolen.

- Forbid your dog from hanging his head out the window; flying debris can injure his eyes and ears.

- Never drive with the windows open enough so that the dog could fall or jump out. An excellent investment are window guards — open steel devices that are held in place by the pressure of rolling up the windows. They let your dog get air without having to stick his head out the window.

- If you will be taking your dog on long trips, take water along and stop at least every couple of hours to walk the dog.

- Be sure you have the dog's collar, identification tag, and leash on and that the the leash is in your hand before your dog starts to get out of the car.

- Never let your dog ride in the back of a pickup truck. In the event of a quick brake or accident, the dog is certain to be thrown out and injured or killed. He might also have his ears and eyes injured by flying debris and, in hot weather, burn his paws on the hot truck bed. If you have no back seat and no room for your dog in the front seat, leave the dog home. There are harnesses designed just for holding dogs in truck beds, but in the event of a bad accident, the injuries to the dog are certain to be serious.

- Believe it or not, dogs have been seen riding in front of their owners on motorcycles. There's no metal separating the dog from the ground or another car. A human can make a choice about whether or not to subject himself to the increased (and well-documented) risk of injury associated with riding motorcycles, but he or she shouldn't impose that risk on a pet.

## Traveling by Bus, Train, and Airplane

Dogs generally are prohibited from buses and trains, but they are allowed on some airline flights. Some airlines allow tiny dogs to ride in the cabin with their owner in a crate, which must be small enough to go under the seat, just like your carry-on baggage. Some airlines forbid all dogs from the cabin. Larger dogs must be crated, and you must have a specific kind of crate; these dogs are usually put in the cargo section of the airplane, which is not air-conditioned. Certain breeds are sometimes prohibited, such as those with short noses and an inefficient respiratory system, and, if you are traveling to a foreign country, dogs might not even be permitted or they might have to be quarantined for many weeks once you get them there.

In 1989, Washington, D.C., television consumer reporter Lea Thompson gave a startling report on pets that were either lost or had died during airplane flights. She related the heartbreaking story of a couple who listened to their golden retriever, placed in the cargo section beneath their feet, whimper and die from the hot temperature that developed while the plane sat on the runway when the takeoff was delayed. Thompson pointed out that no one really knows how many people have had problems flying their pets; the government agency in charge is the Department of Agriculture, and most pet owners who do encounter problems don't know enough to send their complaints there.

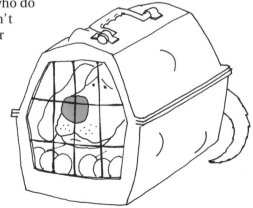

Even sedate, adaptable dogs lucky enough to have a comfortable flight are sure to find an airplane ride a terrifying experience. Unless you can drive and take your dog with you, he's probably better off left at home with a sitter or in a carefully chosen kennel. Puppies, elderly dogs, and dogs with chronic medical conditions may especially suffer if flown on an airplane.

If for some reason you must fly your dog, take a flight that is nonstop and fly your pet only at times when the weather is cool at the place of departure and arrival. Educate yourself carefully about flying by talking to local humane society representatives. Ask which airlines seem to take the best care of dogs. Don't depend on an airline employee to tell you if a certain carrier takes good care of pets.

An excellent source for information on traveling with your pet is a chapter on traveling in the book *The Dog in Your Life,* by Matthew Margolis and Catherine Swan.

## CHAPTER 5

# THE POLITE DOG

*Obedience Training and Handling
Common Behavior Problems*

**M**ost average dog owners don't want their pets trained as well as a police dog or a circus animal. But without some obedience training, you're likely to find your dog's behavior a nuisance.

Picture this: Each time someone comes to visit, you have to battle the dog to keep him away from the door and from jumping up on guests. Family conversations at the dinner table are impossible because the dog is begging and whining all the time. When you're out for a walk, you can't enjoy the scenery or stop and chat with a neighbor because the dog is pulling this way and that, getting his leash wrapped around parking meters and telephone poles.

In contrast, a dog given some well-planned obedience training and follow-up reinforcement can learn to sit and stay in the hallway when someone knocks on the door, to stay away from visiting guests, and to steer clear of your dining room table. He can walk politely down the street next to you, skillfully maneuvering past strangers and other animals. This dog is also less likely to bark incessantly while you are out, to chew things you don't want him to chew, and to wet in the house. This is the sort of dog that will be a real plus in your life, not a pain in the neck.

The major problem dog owners face in training their dogs is limited time and space and a lot of distractions. But if you can devote just 10 to 20 minutes daily to training your dog for several weeks, he can learn to be the most polite pet on the block.

## When Should Obedience Training Be Initiated?

If you have a puppy, some trainers advise waiting until the dog is about six months old before initiating formal training. Other trainers believe training should begin from the first day that you have your dog, assuming she is at least two months old. The best answer for you is probably somewhere in between. As you get to know your dog, you will develop a sense of her attention span and capabilities, and you'll know when it's a good time to begin formalizing her training. In most cases, the earlier the better.

If you have an older dog or even an elderly dog, you really can teach her new tricks. You may have to be more patient, but you'll be amazed at how well she'll respond. Just remember that the way she was treated by previous owners will affect her current behavior, for better or worse.

# Should I Get Professional Dog Training?

If you have never had a dog and have not been around dogs much, it's probably wise to sign up for a community dog obedience class, which generally is inexpensive. You'll not only have the benefit of professional instruction, but you'll get to meet other dog owners and share their experiences. Group classes will help your dog become accustomed to being around lots of other people and dogs, which is especially important for urban dogs. If you like this option, be sure your dog has had all the necessary immunizations before starting obedience classes.

Individual lessons also are available, but they are more expensive, and your dog doesn't have the benefit of being around other people and dogs.

You can successfully train and socialize the dog yourself; all you need is some education. And, if you initiate training and get the feeling it isn't working out, you always have the option of signing up for a class or hiring someone to give you individual lessons.

This chapter will give you the basics of training. There is also a wide variety of books available at bookstores and libraries devoted solely to training if you want more information. When selecting a book, look for one that promotes a humane approach to dog training and that recognizes the fact that different dogs require different handling. An excellent choice would be any of the books featuring the methods of Matthew Margolis. There are also videos out on how to train dogs.

The only time you should not attempt to train the dog yourself, even with instruction from a book, is if you have a dog of a breed associated with aggression or a dog of any breed already exhibiting aggressive behavior, such as the dog that nips and growls at you when you try to correct him. These dogs need careful training and socialization, and few average owners are equipped to handle them alone.

# How to Select a Professional Trainer

Do not assume that anyone who calls himself a dog trainer is qualified. Virtually anyone can hang up a shingle and call himself a trainer, and there are some trainers who can do more damage than good using inhumane training methods. Some people also call themselves animal behaviorists, and they, too, may not be qualified to train dogs. Phyllis Wright, vice-president of companion animals for the Humane Society of the United States (and a former dog trainer herself), says that, even if a trainer belongs to professional organizations, it's no guarantee that he or she is qualified or uses humane methods. The only way to check a trainer out is to get recommendations from former clients — four or five of them. Any good trainer should be glad to give you names. Also ask friends and neighbors with dogs. If you talk to enough people, the same names are going to start coming up, and before long you'll have a good idea of who the best and the worst trainers are in your area.

Once you have a specific trainer in mind and have asked for references, here are a few more questions to ask:

- Does the trainer have his own dogs, and, if so, how does he or she talk about them? With affection, or coldly? This will give you a feeling for whether the trainer is in the business because he or she likes dogs or just to make a buck.

- Ask if your expectations are the same as the trainer's. If you're only interested in teaching your dog the basic commands, you don't need a trainer who will impose the same standards used for obedience trials. The trainer should strive to make training fun for everyone involved, including the dog.

- Can you attend the trainer's group classes to observe the training methods? Some trainers may not have group sessions to observe, but if they do and they refuse to let you come and see for yourself, you probably shouldn't use those trainers.

- Do they emphasize teaching you how to train your dog? A dog trained by a trainer will obey the trainer, but when you get her home, she probably won't obey you.

This is a good reason why you should not use a trainer who wants to work with your dog when you are not there, or who wants to take your dog to his or her home for training. In addition, without being present you cannot protect the dog against inhumane treatment.

- Does the trainer advocate forcefully hitting dogs, or does he or she emphasize negative instead of positive reinforcement? Does he or she use shortcut training — like shock collars for barking dogs? If the answer to any of these questions is yes, don't use this trainer.

- If you want individual training, ask if you can sign up for only one session to see how it goes. Be leery of trainers who insist that you commit to several classes and pay up front. You can always schedule more classes once you decide that you like a trainer and the methods used.

- If you are seeking professional help for a specific problem, such as aggression, the mark of a good trainer will be requiring that you first take your dog to the veterinarian for a checkup to rule out any physical problems that might be contributing to the problem.

Here are two examples of methods used by dog trainers that fall into the unnecessary and potentially harmful category; they also demonstrate that dog owners often know what's best for their own dogs:

**1)** Forcing a successfully housebroken puppy to remain in the house so long that he wets, so that the owner can punish the dog and reinforce housebreaking. The owner of this dog felt that this method was unnecessary and might hinder the positive training already accomplished; she told the trainer, "No thanks, and good-bye." Continued use of positive reinforcement has produced a friendly, well-behaved, and housebroken dog.

**2)** Correcting a puppy that pulled ahead on the leash by "popping" the dog off all four feet with the jerk of a choke collar. This trainer "practiced on logs" in her backyard. The owner feared the dog might be physically harmed and did not use that trainer again. Lots of practice walking and use of a firm but gentle corrective jerk with a choke collar worked just fine.

## Training Equipment

Sturdy, safe equipment is a must. Urban dog owners especially need collars and leashes that won't break, so that their dogs can't dart off into traffic. Ask for guidance from the people at the pet supply store you use and check carefully to see that the stitching in equipment is secure and that metal clasps are sturdy.

### Collars

Put a collar on your dog as soon as you get him, so that he gets used to it. Be especially sure the collar fits properly; it should not be so large that the dog can catch it on something and choke, but it should be roomy enough so that you can get about two fingers underneath. A general rule of thumb is that the collar should be two inches longer than the circumference of the dog's neck.

Generally, either nylon or leather collars are recommended. If you have a puppy, keep in mind that they grow fast and that you'll have to replace the collar frequently; the size should be checked every two weeks. You might want to start out with nylon, which is usually cheaper than leather. Feel the collar carefully with your hands to determine if it's soft enough to be comfortable for your dog.

If you have a large, boisterous dog that is a bit hard to handle, you can buy a metal chain collar. Traditionally, these have been called "choke" collars and have been used by giving quick, firm jerks to get the dog's attention. But there has been concern that jerking the dog's neck might physically damage him, and many owners find that jerking isn't even necessary to train their dog. If you do use a chain or choke collar and feel it's necessary to use jerks, never jerk so hard that the dog's head is pulled up or so that the front feet leave the ground. And don't slowly strangle the dog with any collar. A chain or choke collars must be well made to ensure that it won't break in two, and it must be replaced with the dog's regular collar at all other times, because the links in it can easily catch on something and choke your dog to death.

Your dog should have his rabies tag and an identification tag on his regular collar, attached securely by using a pair of pliers.

## Leashes

A leash should last for many years, so invest in a good leather one that's easy to hold on to in case your dog ever tries to take off. A six-foot length is good for your everyday leash; you can gather it up easily so it's not too long while you are walking with the dog, but it will give you some leeway if the dog needs to walk several feet away to relieve herself.

A very long leash — 20 to 30 feet — isn't essential, but it can be a useful training aid for teaching your dog some of the commands and can be used by urban owners to help exercise their dogs safely outdoors. Since this leash will not be used as often as the dog's regular leash, an inexpensive nylon version with a sturdy clasp should be adequate. Be aware that, in some urban areas, the leash laws prohibit use of a leash longer than six feet, so you may have to limit the areas where you use this piece of equipment.

Start getting your dog used to her leash by putting it on her for a few minutes at a time; let her walk around with it on while you watch to make sure she doesn't get it caught on anything, then take it off.

# Training Your Dog Yourself

One family member should conduct the training sessions. After the dog is responding well, carefully instruct other family members about the methods used — the command words, how the dog was positioned and praised — then have other family members work with the dog. As you begin training, remember this: Be positive, patient, and consistent.

Positive first and foremost means using positive reinforcement. The dog is taught a command and is rewarded primarily with praise by the owner. Dogs like to please their owners, and they will want to obey again and again to get more of that good stuff — praise.

In fact, all contact you have with your dog should be with positive reinforcement in mind. You want him to form positive associations with his name, with the commands, and with your voice and your hands. For instance, always use your dog's name in a positive manner — don't call the dog's name before issuing a "No." And don't tell the dog to "come" and then punish him, because, the next time around, he'll be hesitant to obey; instead, you go to the dog to correct him. Your voice should almost always sound friendly with the dog, and when you do issue a "No!" it should be stern compared to your regular voice, but you shouldn't be screaming. If you never hit your dog with your hands and instead use your hands only to pet the dog and gently position him during training, he will welcome your touch, not avoid it.

That you should be patient when training your dog seems obvious, but many owners find their tempers flaring after the first few sessions if the dog doesn't catch on. As you become tense, so does the dog. Don't try to work with your dog if you are feeling impatient and irritable. Have a cup of tea or coffee, relax, improve your frame of mind, and then have your training session.

## Why You Shouldn't Bully the Dog

You'll see dog owners who scream and yell and even hit their dogs if the dogs don't learn fast enough or if they disobey the owner. Contrary to the advice of the best dog trainers, these owners cannot be convinced of the benefits of positive reinforcement. They seem to feel that the dog is "getting the best of them"; they can't stand the thought that they are unable to control this subhuman creature, the dog. The owner approaches every training session as though it were a battle to be won.

But bullying makes dogs fearful, and it only complicates the training process. The dog is given a command, and then, instead of that simple reaction to obey so that she can be rewarded, the dog is distracted by a rush of fear that she'll get clobbered, either verbally or physically. Her instincts are probably telling her to run and hide under the coffee table. And a fearful dog is more likely to develop behavior problems. She could end up being a biter because she's afraid, or so timid you can't do anything with her because she hides at every opportunity to avoid the "bad thing" — getting yelled at or hit.

Bullying your dog to train her is also exhausting for the owner; it takes a lot more effort, because the dog just isn't going to respond as well as she will to positive reinforcement.

Phyllis Wright puts it this way: "If you can't control yourself, you can't control the dog."

## How to Plan a Training Schedule

Plan a training routine that suits your schedule; don't create an unrealistic plan that's doomed to failure. You might want to begin with five minutes in the morning and five in the evening, or with one 10- to 20-minute session every evening. If your schedule is erratic and you have to do a session one day in the morning and one the next day at midnight, that's fine. The important thing is to practice daily, or at least five or six times a week, for several weeks, until you see that the dog has caught on and that the commands are becoming second nature to him.

## Where to Train the Dog
## and How to Incorporate Social Skills

Initiation of training indoors is practical and usually preferable for urban owners. Outside, there are likely to be so many distractions that your dog can't concentrate. Begin in a room without other people around. After your dog begins to catch on to the first command or two, practice inside with someone else around. Then, if he's gotten the okay from the veterinarian to be taken outside, start taking him out of the house to practice. Pick a place and time without too many distractions — don't take him out the first time to a place near road crews using jackhammers, for instance. Then start varying the places you take him, and *gradually increase the distractions.* Some dogs taught obedience exclusively in one place will not perform the commands in another place, and urban dogs especially need to be versatile.

If you are unable to take your dog outside for training, then you probably have a tiny dog anyway. Socialize him by progressing from training alone with him to training in the house with other people around. When you do go out, take the dog with you, even if it's only down the hall to get the mail or to the laundry room.

Once training is well under way and your dog has been housebroken, you can begin to think about giving the dog increased freedom in the house. Increase his space gradually; leave two puppy-proofed rooms open to the dog instead of one. Do it first when you are at home — you'll keep an eye on the dog, but won't be supervising as carefully as before. When the dog has behaved himself in the new room of freedom, praise him highly when you come in. Next, try leaving him home alone for a very short time in his two new rooms, praising him when you come home if he's been good. Repeat these short sessions of absence several times before leaving the dog alone for longer periods of time. And, if the dog does demonstrate inappropriate behavior like chewing, you'll find solutions later in this chapter.

THE GUILT-FREE DOG OWNER'S GUIDE

# Teaching the Commands

Put the leash on the dog and start by teaching one command at a time, one way at a time. Some dogs will learn a new command after just three or four tries; others may require 25 tries. Some dogs respond the second after you give a command, and some take several seconds. When your dog catches on to one command and can do it consistently several times in a row, add another command to your training repertoire. Before you begin each training session, think carefully about what you are going to teach your dog and how. You must give your dog clear messages — one word or command at a time and clear, well-defined positioning of your hands. You must be consistent, or else the dog won't be able to catch on.

Generally, you can expect your dog to learn to sit in about a week. Most dogs can learn all the basic commands in several weeks and, after one month of consistent training, will respond 80 percent of the time.

Some owners find that the only way they can get their dog to obey is by bribing the dog with a treat for each command. Former trainer Phyllis Wright thinks that giving your dog little tidbits in addition to verbal and physical praise helps get the dog's attention and can aid in the training process. Just try to avoid letting your dog get so dependent on treats that he won't perform without them, since you can't always have a treat handy when you want your dog to obey. As the dog learns, gradually replace the treats with verbal and physical praise alone and use treats for obedience sparingly.

Some dogs won't respond to a seriously conducted training session, but will obey if you act like you're playing with them. Use whatever works!

## Sit

Stand next to your dog on his right side, holding the leash in your right hand as though you were going to take him for walk. Gather the leash up so there's only about a foot between your hand and the dog's neck. Then, at the same time, gently pull up on the leash with your right hand while you gently press the dog's rear end down with your left hand, and say "Sit." As soon as you get your dog into the sit position, reward the dog with lots of praise: "Good boy! Good boy!" and several pats. The leash must be loose so the collar doesn't get too tight; avoid strangling the dog by keeping your elbows next to your ribs.

If your dog doesn't catch on after several tries, try the same maneuver, but, instead of pulling up on the leash with your right hand, try lifting the dog's chin with your right hand. If your dog seems to understand this way better, stick to it.

## Down

With your dog in the sit position, get on your knees next to the dog, and say "Down" as you gently pull the dog's front feet out so that he has to lie down. As soon as you get him down, praise him. What you want to avoid is a struggle to get the dog down; this will make him uncomfortable and less likely to obey. Be especially careful to keep your voice friendly and gentle, because most dogs will find this new maneuver somewhat disconcerting. Keep it fun!

Some owners find they can teach their dog this command simply by holding a treat on the floor under the dog's nose and, with the other hand, patting the floor.

## Stay

Put your dog into the sit position, then slowly bring your hand around in front of the dog's face so that you are showing the dog the palm of your hand. As you do this, say "Stay," then walk out and around so that you are about a foot in front of your dog, facing him. If the dog keeps getting up, try holding up the leash and your dog's head with your left hand as you signal with your right hand and walk around in front of the dog. The goal here is to get the dog to stay — if only for a second or two — just enough time so that you can praise the dog and help him get the idea of what you want him to do. Once your dog catches on, gradually increase the distance you stand away from the dog during this exercise and the time the dog is expected to stay.

Your dog is more likely to catch on if you maintain eye contact with him. If the dog begins to act restless, he's going to break the stay position, so try to praise him before he moves. Phyllis Wright says, "I'd rather praise the dog ten times than correct him once."

Next, begin practicing the stay command with the dog in the down position and with the dog standing.

## Come

You've already been teaching your dog this command each time you gesture or talk to your dog and he comes to you. Now you are going to incorporate it into your formal training sessions. Gesture to your dog in the way you've been doing to get him to come to you — perhaps you pat your thighs as you give an encouraging "Fido!" Start making more deliberate use of the word "Come" and use the dog's name. You want your dog to learn that he's now going to come to you anytime you issue this word. Practice calling the dog from different areas of the house — go into another room and call the dog. Give lots of praise when the dog gets to you.

THE GUILT-FREE DOG OWNER'S GUIDE

If your dog is having trouble with "Come," try using a long leash and gently pull the dog toward you while you say the word. Another useful method is to run backward. The dog is more likely to follow you.

## Heel

First think about how you will hold the leash. The end with the loop should be in your right hand, with either your thumb or your whole hand through the loop and with the rest of your hand grasping the part of the leash right under the loop. Use whichever holding method you feel gives you the most secure hold, and, if you're using a six-foot leash, gather it up a bit more in your right hand, so that the middle of the leash isn't touching the ground but isn't pulling on the dog either. With your left palm down, grasp the portion of the leash that is about halfway between the dog's neck and your right hand.

Start by walking around the house with the dog on your left side. Say "Heel" as you begin walking, in a tone of voice indicating that this is great fun. Walk around in such a way that you'll be making turns only to the right. Your goal is to get the dog to learn to walk next to your left leg without having to apply tension on the leash. The dog's nose should be just a little ahead of your left leg; he should be back far enough so that he can see which way you are going to go. If the dog is catching on, begin practicing wide left turns.

Pulling ahead is a common problem, especially when you begin taking the dog outside for walks. Let the dog pull out ahead, and, when the dog hits the end of the line, give a quick jerk of the leash — jerk and release! — with your left hand, as you make either a right, 90-degree turn or a 180-degree turn and start walking. The jerk is a way of saying "Hey! Listen up!" The turn is giving the message that the dog has got to stay by your side if he's to keep up with you.

If the dog won't walk next to you and lags behind, try coaxing him playfully and, if that doesn't work, give a quick jerk to get him going. Give lots of praise the second he begins to move with you.

Practice and the gradual conditioning of your dog to distractions is particularly important when you are teaching your dog to heel; this is the command that you'll be using most outdoors so that you can maneuver around neighbors, strangers, and other dogs. When loud noises occur, as they are likely to, don't make a big deal about them; say at most "It's okay," and just keep going, so your dog learns to keep going, too. If you talk pleasantly to your dog while you walk with him, it will make him more at ease and make the walks more fun for him.

Some owners find that, if they praise the dog too soon after a correction for heel, the dog can't distinguish which behavior the owner wants

— the wrong position or the correct one. After correcting the dog, wait until he's been walking in the correct position for about 15 or 20 seconds before praising him.

## Integrate the Commands into Everyday Life

As your dog learns each command, begin using them and rewarding the dog at times other than in formal training sessions. Tell the dog down/stay, for instance, when you are eating dinner or you have company. If the dog gets up and moves away, go get the dog in a pleasant manner, put him on his leash, then bring him back to where you want him and put him in the down/stay position. Reward him after he's kept that position for a length of time within his capabilities.

Don't, however, ask the dog to obey unreasonable commands; you can't, for instance, expect a four-month-old puppy with one week of training to remain in a down/stay position for ten minutes or even five. If you can get him to down/stay for 30 to 60 seconds, that dog is doing very well. Reward him before he has a chance to take off!

## Backsliding

This isn't a command, but it's what dogs will do if their lessons are not reinforced continually. You may have completed your training sessions but find your dog starting to ignore your commands. Ask yourself why. Have you simply not had the occasion to use the commands every day? Refresher sessions are needed; a few times weekly might be enough to maintain the dog's obedient behavior.

## Don't Expect Perfection

Just like individual people, some dogs are good at some things but not at others, and some dogs seem to have aversions you can't explain. Your dog, for instance, might obey all the commands you've taught him, but for some reason he won't down/stay in a certain spot in the house. Unless there's some crucial reason he must learn to obey there, don't force the issue. Perhaps the floor in that part of the house makes him uncomfortable. One urban owner who taught her dog to sit at every curbside outdoors found that her dog suddenly one day wouldn't. She finally figured out that the scorching hot pavement was burning the dog's improperly cut tail stub, which touched the ground when he sat.

Some dogs have been mistreated by previous owners, which might explain their resistance to certain situations and commands. Decide what's really important, and drop what isn't.

## Behavior Problems Common to Confined Dogs

Bad behavior is not an acceptable reason to get rid of a dog. The exception to that rule might be the dog that seems to have gone "mad" and acts wildly aggressive, which is a rare occurrence.

Each year, hundreds of thousands of dogs are dumped or destroyed because their owners could not cope with their behavior. You'll hear stories about how the dog dug a hole in the wall or chewed the corner off of a $3,000 area rug. The owners who get rid of their dogs almost always say that they "tried everything," but, more often than not, the truth is that they made only a halfhearted effort. First, they didn't try to prevent the behavior from happening. Or they tried a remedy or two, but only gave it a day or two to work and then gave up. The other great pitfall is inconsistency, trying a remedy a day here and a day there — a method that is certain to fail.

The point here is that dogs are being dumped and destroyed because of their owners' failure to tackle the problem in an efficient, effective manner. Now it may be — as it is for many typically busy dog owners — that your schedule prevents you from doing what you need to do to correct the dog's behavior. That's a common and perfectly understandable problem. But it isn't a reason to get rid of the dog, because there are solutions to this problem, too!

Most of the behavior problems common to confined dogs appear below. If your dog is demonstrating any of them, first start out at the veterinarian's office to see if he or she can pinpoint the cause, such as a nutritional deficiency, which leads to chewing in some dogs. If your dog gets a clean bill of health, next try to figure out behavioral reasons why your dog is demonstrating a certain behavior. Then start trying the remedies that seem most appropriate and that you can use effectively. For some dogs, one remedy might work. Other dogs might require you to use all the remedies. Some dogs respond more quickly than others; some will start behaving and then backslide. This is all normal. If the problem is your schedule, read on.

## Chewing (Sometimes Combined with Digging)

Puppies usually chew because they are teething; chewing helps their teeth break through the gums. Puppies start getting their permanent teeth around four months of age, when their front teeth come in. Teething continues until nine or ten months, when the molars come in. Older dogs in good health who chew may be bored, anxious, or both.

The bored dog chews because she has too much energy and not enough outlets. And what do you expect her to do? She can only sleep so much. She can't get interested in a television program, read a book, do housework, or call a friend on the phone and chat. Unless you've spent a lot of time teaching your dog what she can and cannot chew, how can you expect her to know the difference between her nylon chew toy and the leg on the table?

The dog known as the "spite chewer" — the one that seems to chew to get revenge for being left alone — generally is the dog that will chew as soon as you leave, even if you've spent all day playing with her and exercising her. The more likely reason this dog chews is because she's upset that you've left her. Behaviorists call this *separation anxiety*. When you go out, the dog has no idea whether you will return in one minute, one hour, or ever. These dogs need to learn that it is routine that you'll return. Let's put it another way: *your returning needs to become a habit to the dog.*

### Your Reaction to Chewing

When you come home and find that your dog has destroyed something, a sharp "No!" is in order if you catch him in the act; after that, ignore the dog for perhaps five to ten minutes. You don't want him to associate attention from you with the act of chewing, even if it's negative attention.

If you do not catch the dog in the act, don't scold but, again, don't give the dog any attention. Some trainers advise that you pick up the chewed object or look at it, act as though you are displeased, curse to yourself, and go about some other business in the house.

Some dogs will cower when you come in if they've done something "bad," even if you don't catch them in the act. This may make the owner think the dog knows what he did and, thus, should be punished. This behavior could, however, mean that the dog is so often scolded or punished upon the owner's return that he is beginning to associate the owner's return with something unpleasant and will cower whenever the front door opens. Even if the dog *is* beginning to get the sense he did something he shouldn't have, he doesn't have the brainpower to put it all together — "I chewed her new shoes up to get even with her for leaving me, and now she's going to give me attention by punishing me." If dogs could reason that well, they'd be able to reason that it made more sense not to chew!

Keep your perspective. Granted, it's pretty upsetting if a dog destroys something valuable, but you should have protected it in the first place. And if the dog does ruin something that you couldn't move, like the molding around the doorway, it can be replaced cheaply. Remember that, in many dogs, chewing is a behavior that is outgrown either as they finish the teething stage or as they finally begin to adjust, to feel secure in their new home, and as they get some training.

### Remedies for Chewing

Here are some remedies you can use, no matter what your dog's age or the cause of chewing. Use as few or as many of these options as are necessary; start with the least drastic, then work your way up.

- Puppy-proof your dog's space as described in the puppy-proofing section in Chapter 2. Don't give the dog unsupervised access to another room until she's behaving well in the first room (and she's housebroken or paper-trained), and puppy-proof each room you give her until you feel certain she'll behave in that room. Block off valuable furniture and use deterrent sprays for weeks or months if necessary. If you've got an expensive area rug down, roll it up and put it in another room if you have to. Do it before the dog has a chance to misbehave, so that you establish positive rather than negative behavior.

- Provide your dog with lots of safe chew toys.

- If you usually have the television or radio on when you are home, leave them on when you leave; the dog may feel more at ease.

THE POLITE DOG

- Initiate obedience training and stick to it.

- Increase the dog's exercise daily and leave her with food in her tummy when you go out; she's more likely to sleep than chew.

- Take the time to correct your dog when you are home. Put some inappropriate objects on the floor, such as a shoe and perhaps a pad of notebook paper, and an appropriate object, such as the dog's chew. If the dog goes for the shoe, give her a firm "No," take the shoe away, and replace it with the dog's chew. Praise the dog when she chews appropriate items. Keep doing this until the dog begins to form the habit of chewing only the things you give her to chew. Do not, however, hand the dog an inappropriate item to chew and then scold her.

- If you think the cause of chewing is separation anxiety, gradually condition the dog to your comings and goings. The word "gradual" here is imperative — don't leave the dog alone for one minute in the morning, then for several hours that afternoon. Start out with just minutes away every day for several days, then increase the time to perhaps ten minutes several times daily, then to 20 minutes, and so on until you get up to about one or two hours without the dog having chewed something inappropriate. Return before the dog has a chance to do something bad, so that you can praise her for being good. If she backslides, then you should backtrack in the training.

- Be sure that when you leave and return you do so calmly and matter-of-factly; the dog shouldn't think that your leaving is a big deal.

- Foster your dog's independence in the house. Give her lots of love and attention, but not all the time; if she goes off to another room or a corner to nap, leave her alone. Take her out often for rides in the car and for walks around the neighborhood or in your building.

If these remedies don't seem to work or if your work schedule prevents you from using them consistently and you are beginning to feel that you cannot tolerate finding any more items destroyed in your home, you need to consider dog day care or a pet sitter — action to prevent the dog from demonstrating bad behavior — at least until she adjusts and/or outgrows the chewing stage and until you have time to initiate regular training. If your pet seems to be chewing only if you leave her alone for more than three hours, then have someone come in every two hours. If you find that your dog doesn't chew if she's had a good exercise session in the morning and you don't have time to exercise her, hire someone to do it. Consult Chapter 6 on Dog Schedules, Sitters, and Kennels for more information.

THE GUILT-FREE DOG OWNER'S GUIDE

## Barking

Barking is natural, and a dog that barks only when strangers come around the house should be commended, not punished, especially in an urban area where everyone lives with the threat of crime. Some dogs will bark to warn their owner and, once the owner acknowledges the dog's message with an "Okay, I hear it," they will stop barking.

Problem barking occurs when a dog barks nonstop and the neighbors complain. Some dogs bark incessantly because they are "hyper" and overreact to every little sound around them; others may bark because they are anxious that their owner left them. Some of the toy dogs are notorious barkers.

### Remedies for Problem Barking

First you've got to figure out why the dog is barking, and that can be difficult. Ask a cooperative neighbor to help you try and pinpoint the cause. Does she notice that the dog is really howling, not barking, as though he's miserable you are gone? Then the dog may need conditioning to your absence. Or is it only the trash collectors who set him off? Some trainers advise leaving on a tape recorder while you are out to try and figure out what makes the dog bark. And some trainers have found that, occasionally, the dog isn't barking at all — the problem is a kooky neighbor complaining just to complain!

- Tell your dog "No!" if he barks wildly when you are home, and, if necessary, restrict him by keeping him with you and on his leash so you can issue "Noes." Don't then pet the dog to soothe him, which might give him a contradictory message, but if he starts to refrain from barking at certain sounds, praise and pet him for being quiet.

- Mask out sounds by leaving on the television set or the radio. If you live in one of those apartments with a big crack under the front door, cover it with a heavy towel so the dog is less likely to hear footsteps.

- Eliminate visuals that might contribute to barking. If your dog barks when he's looking out the window at the people going by, shut the shades so he can't see out.

- Increase the exercise the dog gets and leave him with food in his tummy, especially before you go out, so that he's more likely to sleep while you aren't home.

- If you think the dog is barking because he's anxious about you leaving him, condition him to your absences as outlined above under the remedies for chewing.

- If none of these tactics works, you'll have to try conditioning the dog not to bark. Pretend you are going out, stay near the front door, and wait for the dog to bark. Then, as soon as he starts, come in quickly and tell him "No!" Do this over and over.

- Hire a carefully chosen trainer to help you condition your dog not to bark if you don't have the time, although you'll have to reinforce the lessons and work with the dog when you are home.

- Get a pet sitter or dog day care if you can't make any of these other remedies work, until you can initiate some effective training and conditioning.

> **TIP**
> Behaviorist Stephen C. Rafe has developed a tape called kalMMusic that might help reduce problem barking or relax dogs who become anxious over their owner's absence. See the product list in the back of the book for information on ordering.

## Jumping Up

A lot of dog owners let their dogs jump up on them and then expect the dog to refrain from jumping up on guests. It's difficult to have it both ways, so when your dog jumps up on you, tell him "No!" and walk away. That way, he'll get the message that he isn't going to get any attention with this maneuver. You might also ask a friend or relative who knows the dog to come over to do the same exercise to help train the dog.

The reason dogs jump up is to say hello. Sometimes the easiest solution is for the owner or guest to squat, have the dog sit, and let the dog get the "Hello" over with.

## Charging the Front Door

It can seem like a blessing when you have an unwelcome solicitor at the door, but when it's one of the neighbors or your grandmother visiting, a dog who barks and jumps at the door and at guests can be a real nuisance. Try to prevent this behavior by teaching your dog from the first day you have her that she is to sit and stay several feet back from the door when the bell rings. The leash can be used to help the dog learn to obey.

If you've already got a charger on your hands, try the technique recommended by Job Michael Evans in his book *The Evans Guide for Civilized City Canines*. Pull down on the dog's collar or leash and say "No!" Then pull up on the collar or leash, tell the dog to sit, and command the

THE GUILT-FREE DOG OWNER'S GUIDE

dog to stay. Have friends and relatives come over so you can practice this. If the dog doesn't get the message, only open the door halfway and, if necessary, keep closing the door in the visitor's face until the dog obeys. "The point you want your dog to get is that persons are not admitted until the dog is seated and under control," Evans says.

Evans even advises conducting "dry runs" with no one at the door. You open and close the door as though someone were there and even ring the bell or knock yourself. This author and her dog can testify that this method works!

## Mounting

This behavior is more common among male dogs, but there are female dogs that have been known to "mount," and, if they are not corrected, they will continue with this behavior. Divert the dog's attention to another activity. Don't let the dog form the habit.

## Begging

If you feed the dog from your table, she won't be able to understand why it's okay to beg sometimes and not at other times. It's best never to feed your dog from the table. If your dog begs, give her a "No" and ignore her. Continue with normal family dinnertime conversation and continue to ignore the dog, even if the dog is driving you nuts whining. Eventually, she should get the message that she has nothing to gain from begging.

## Nipping or Biting

Nipping by puppies during play sessions or gnawing on your hand while they are teething rarely is cause for concern, but you don't want the dog to learn that using his teeth is acceptable behavior. Tell him "No," and if necessary walk away and go to another activity, so that the dog gets no attention for using his teeth.

If, however, you find yourself with a dog who growls, nips, or bites in an unfriendly manner when you try to correct him, or at any other time, seek help from a professional trainer. The trainer should first require a visit to the veterinarian, especially for the dog that has been friendly and then begins to nip or bite. Be sure that you get a trainer who hashad considerable experience treating aggressive dogs with humane methods. The trainer should use different methods for different dogs — a dog that bites because he's afraid, for instance, should be treated differently than the aggressive biter. Also consider whether it's possible that someone has been abusing or mistreating your dog. Until your dog is trained and under control, keep him away from other people and dogs to prevent an incident.

## CHAPTER 6

# DOG SCHEDULES, SITTERS, AND KENNELS

If you are a typically busy person who must leave your dog alone most days while you are at work, let's hope you're lucky enough to find yourself with a pet that settles right into your lifestyle. This kind of dog seems content to loaf around the house all day while you are at work. He doesn't howl, chew, or bark and is able to hold his urine or uses his newspaper if that's what he's been taught to do. He's lively and affectionate when you return. He acts like a happy dog. But this is an unusual scenario, especially if you are starting out with a puppy or an energetic adult dog.

More often than not, dog owners find that their work schedules make meeting the daily needs of their dogs difficult. With some thought and planning, though, you can devise a schedule for your dog so that his needs are met. It may require changing your routine a bit or, if you can't do that, hiring someone to help you. But making this effort means that you'll stop worrying about your dog when you are out and that you'll be able to enjoy his companionship when you're with him.

Besides solving everyday problems, you may also need to arrange for someone to care for your dog when you travel.

## Dog Schedules

What is a long day for a dog? Although some dogs can remain at home all day alone, many cannot, and the reasons vary widely. Perhaps your dog is housebroken, but his bladder dictates that he must be taken outside every four hours, whereas you work an eight-hour day. Or perhaps your dog simply cannot tolerate isolation. Isolation is a major problem among confined dogs. Some of them chew, bark, and generally act wild when you leave them alone, especially if they have not adjusted to their new home and if their owners haven't had time to train them. In other dogs the symptoms of isolation might be moping and lethargy.

Even if your dog doesn't demonstrate any symptoms of problem behavior and is allowed to use newspaper in the house to relieve himself, it's not fair to leave him cooped up in the house all day, every day, without a break, unless you will give him lots of attention at almost all other times. Eight hours is the absolute limit the dog should be left alone — and that's assuming you have a female that uses paper in the house or a dog that you are sure can comfortably hold urine that long. Certainly, some kind of attention every four to five hours is preferable.

THE GUILT-FREE DOG OWNER'S GUIDE

Here are some examples of the ways in which you can schedule activities for your dog to meet his needs for attention, exercise, and relief:

- If your dog must spend all day alone, he will have a happier day if he begins it with a play and exercise session, then some food, and if on most days he can look forward to the same routine as soon as you come home, staying with you until the next morning.

- Some dogs that cannot tolerate being alone all day will do fine if they get a midday walk or indoor play session followed by some loving attention and a treat, especially if you aren't a morning person and can't fit in play and exercise before your workday. To accomplish this, consider coming home for lunch; it's a lot cheaper than eating out. Or, if you don't work close to home, consider going to work early or staying late in exchange for a longer lunch hour. It's a great midday break for you and your dog, and it will spare you from one rush hour!

- Another alternative is to hire someone to walk the dog or play with him indoors for half an hour midday. Or rotate: You come home for lunch three days a week and hire someone else to do it the other two workdays.

- If your dog is howling, barking incessantly, chewing, or demonstrating other destructive behavior the minute you leave, and you aren't able to succeed with any of the remedies outlined in Chapter 5, your dog may need day care, at least until he adjusts and you can institute some regular training. How to find a sitter is discussed later in this chapter.

- If you think your dog is lonely, or common sense tells you that the dog is being left alone too much, and dog day care isn't a feasible idea, consider getting another pet to provide company for the dog. An alternative is to find another neighbor with a dog that would also benefit from companionship. Let the dogs get to know each other and leave them together during the day. Make sure the neighbor's dog is well cared for and has had all necessary immunizations.

- Don't forget your dog's nightlife. If you will be at work all day and are planning to be out all evening socializing, rushing home at 6 P.M. to feed the dog and take him out quickly isn't adequate. The dog should be exercised and have a fun, unrushed play session. Remember that, for the dog, you are his life. On evenings you can't devote an hour or two to your dog before going back out, get a dog walker or sitter to do it for you.

# Pet Sitters

Whether you need a pet sitter to help with everyday scheduling problems or to care for your dog while you travel, there are several arrangements that can be made. Some sitters will come to your home and stay there with the dog. Some will come to your home just long enough to feed and exercise the dog, then leave, and some will keep your dog in their homes for you.

If the purpose of a sitter is daily dog care while you are at work, most dogs will adjust to the sitter's home if they are well treated there and go regularly. If you are traveling, the ideal situation is the live-in pet sitter, since your dog will be upset anyway that you are gone and she will be most comfortable in her own home. There are owners who leave their dogs home alone while they travel and have someone come in daily just to check on the dog and feed and exercise her, but this plan could spell disaster if your dog becomes ill or injures herself while she's alone for long periods. And, if you really want your dog to be happy while you are gone, you will want to see that she gets attention most of the time you are absent.

The easiest way to find a pet sitter is through a professional pet-sitting service. But they are expensive. Some charge $9 or $10 just for one visit to your home daily; the dog is walked for perhaps 15 to 20 minutes, and your plants are watered and the mail is taken in if you wish. According to an owner of one of these companies, the major reason for the high cost is the premiums these companies pay to insure their employees, who generally are also bonded. Obviously, most average dog owners cannot afford these services on a regular basis.

A more economical way to find someone to care for your pet is by word of mouth; it takes more time and effort on your part, but it can be done if you are determined. Urban dog owners in particular have an advantage; they usually belong to a homeowners or condominium or tenants association, which provides the opportunity to meet neighbors, make contacts, and get recommendations. Start asking other neighbors if they know of any responsible persons in your building or neighborhood whom they think would make responsible pet sitters.

Consider a senior citizen. Some older persons have lost their dogs but, sadly, do not get another pet because they fear the dog will outlive them. These neighbors might really enjoy earning a few extra dollars for pet sitting. If money is tight for you, consider bartering; perhaps you could help the neighbor with grocery shopping in exchange for providing companionship for your pet while you are at work or traveling. This arrangement is best for dogs who are small, are easy to handle, and are paper-trained and don't have to be taken outside.

If your dog is boisterous or hard to handle and needs to be taken outside regularly, a major concern will be finding someone to help who will not let the dog get away and run into traffic. Ask neighbors if they know of any responsible high school students in your building or neighborhood. The ideal situation is getting a responsible teenager who is anxious to earn a little extra money and who has a responsible parent keeping an eye on the teen.

Another source for sitters is the local university or college; most urban areas have several of them, and, either by word of mouth or the student employment service, you might be able to find someone who would jump at the chance to get out of the dormitory and into a private home to study and keep your dog company. The resident advisors in the dorms — older students in charge of groups of younger students — might be good people to ask for names and recommendations. Generally, they'll know which students are wild, crazy, and irresponsible and which ones are more studious and stable. If you will be using the student while you travel, the student could attend classes or perhaps go to work while pet sitting, which will generally lower the fee you must pay.

Don't overlook the receptionists and technicians who work at your veterinarian's office. You probably already know them, and they would be ideal sitters to have, especially if your dog becomes ill while you are traveling.

How much should you pay these people? If you need a sitter only occasionally, for a few hours at a time, find out what the going rate for hourly babysitting is in your area and offer that much or a bit less, unless your dog is really hard to handle. If you need someone all day, every day, or for several days or weeks while you travel, negotiate a flat per diem rate that you can afford.

The other obvious possibility is to use relatives or good friends who like your dog and who may volunteer to keep her for you for free. You may be lucky enough to know other people who adore your dog and will go out of their way to care for the dog in a responsible manner. But there are also friends who might be lax about dog-sitting responsibilities because they feel they are doing you a favor. If you do use friends, be careful not to take advantage of their kindness; reciprocate whenever you can by returning the favor or by thanking them with an appropriate gift. Never take their services for granted.

Before you finalize arrangements for someone to care for your dog, be sure to consider the following:

• Don't commit to a long-term arrangement until you've tried and tested a sitter. Start out by asking the person to sit for only an hour or two at first to see if the dog and the sitter sincerely seem to like each other.

If that goes well, the next time use the sitter for perhaps an evening only. Since you'll want to take care not to offend neighbors or friends, gradually work your way into the arrangement in a way that will enable you to pull out gracefully if it doesn't work out.

- If sitters will be taking your dog outside for walks, go out with them first to make sure that they seem able to handle the dog on a leash, especially if you live in an urban area. And make sure they have no objections to scooping up after your dog!

- Even if a potential sitter is regarded as a highly responsible person, he or she should have had some experience with dogs. People who haven't, believe it or not, won't know when a dog has to be taken out to relieve himself or that dogs should not eat certain plants or be fed chocolate. If the dog sees a cat and tries to bolt while they are outside, these are the people who might become frightened or panic and let the dog dart out into traffic.

- If you use a professional service, it should be recommended by either your veterinarian, humane society representatives, or trusted friends. Ask the service for the names of four or five clients you can call to obtain references. The better services will be willing to make a get-acquainted visit to get to know your pet and to have you fill out forms about the dog's needs.

- Verbally review your dog's needs, even if the sitter has had considerable experience with dogs, and then leave a written list for the sitter. For instance, specify how often the dog needs to be taken outside to relieve himself, when and what he is to be fed, and how frequent and how long the play sessions should be. Don't forget to review and list any medication your dog requires. If you have a live-in sitter while you are out of town, and the sitter will be going out to work or school, make certain that you and the sitter understand and agree on the maximum time the dog can be left alone.

- Before you leave your dog at someone else's home, carefully consider the potential for the dog getting out; dogs that are upset at being left by their owners might try to escape. They have a much greater chance of getting out if they are in a hectic household with children running in and out. If you leave your dog in such a household, express these concerns to the sitters so it will be in their minds, too: "Gee, do you think you'll have trouble keeping the dog from escaping? I mean, he always tries to get out when I'm gone, and you can't tell your kids not to go in and out. . . ." If it's a single retired person with few or no distractions in the household, the dog is probably less likely to get out accidentally.

- If you will be leaving a teenager in your home with the dog, be especially careful to set ground rules. Obviously, if the sitter has a party in your house and things get out of hand, the dog could escape or end up biting someone. Be sure to specify that the teens have no one else in the house while they are sitting for you, or ask that they have only one friend in at a time. If you explain nicely and tell the sitter the reason for this rule, he or she is more likely to comply.

- Observe your dog's reaction to the sitter and his behavior when the sitter leaves. Does he wag his tail and act as though he likes the sitter? Ideally, he will be so happy with the sitter that he won't have missed you much. If you have any reservations about whether a live-in sitter is staying with your dog when he or she is supposed to, have a friend or relative call while you are out to see if the sitter answers. To avoid offending the sitter, the caller can simply say he called to see if everything is okay and to ask if he can be of any help.

## Dog Kennels, Motels, and Hotels

The author knows one dog who so likes a certain kennel that he races in the door, wagging his tail and excitedly looking forward to his stay. That's a tribute to attentive care, but it's a pretty unusual case. Most dogs, especially those who are house pets used to their owner's companionship, are not going to take to kenneling readily, and, because they will be exposed to many other dogs, there is always the risk that they could catch an illness. For some owners, though, kenneling is a good option or perhaps the only option; if you take the time to find a good kennel, your dog could grow to like it there.

Besides kennels, there are similar facilities in some urban areas that are often called pet hotels and motels. Because many urban areas prohibit outdoor kennels due to the noise the dogs create, urban kennels tend to be indoor operations. Some of them even provide dog day care on a regular basis or for dog owners who need occasional help — for instance, on days their homes are being exterminated or painted.

The cost varies widely among all kinds of kennels: some charge as little as $3 daily for day care of small dogs; others might charge $15 daily for a medium-sized dog staying overnight. But the fee (or the presence of brass beds and other fancy dog paraphernalia) does not necessarily mean that your dog will receive good care. So how do you select a good kennel?

First, get recommendations from your veterinarian — he or she may have seen dogs that became ill when they stayed at a certain kennel — or from your local humane society. All good kennels should require verification from your veterinarian that your dog is up-to-date on immunizations, including the one for kennel cough. They should have a veterinarian on call or a nearby emergency clinic that they use.

Ideally, the kennel should have a staff member on the premises 24 hours a day — the janitor doesn't count — and, at the very least, someone coming in overnight to check on the dogs. Dr. Randall Lockwood, director of higher education programs for the Humane Society of the United States, says that if someone isn't on the premises 24 hours a day, he would want to know if the kennel has an alarm to signal dangerous drops or increases in the kennel's temperature, as well as a fire alarm system. If the alarms go off, someone must be able to get to the dogs quickly.

Writing in *The Humane Society News,* Dr. Lockwood and Deborah Salem say that all reputable kennels will welcome a get-acquainted visit and an inspection, so that you can see the facilities and discuss the care provided — which you should do before you leave the dog there. The kennel should be clean and well kept; fences to keep dogs in, for instance, should be in top condition to prevent dogs from escaping. But even more important is the rapport the staff have with the dogs, the authors point out.

Linda Buel, owner of the Rockville Pet Motel outside of Washington, D.C., also emphasizes the importance of human interaction with the dogs, especially urban dogs, because they are house pets dependent on humans for their companionship. The staff should use the dog's name and talk to the dog a lot, not just stick him in a pen to entertain himself, she says.

As important as this interaction, says Linda, is that the kennel be willing and able to provide the dog's regular diet. She has one regular dog customer who will not eat his food unless it's mixed with barbecued chicken from a certain local grocery store, so that's what Linda gives him. On other occasions she might find herself cooking up a beef stew. It may seem silly to some people, but if you don't give the dogs what they are used to, they will refuse to eat, and that could be detrimental to the dogs' health and general well-being, especially since many of her canine clients stay with her for two weeks at a time. She charges by weight, and these special diets are included in the price of kenneling. The dogs are not kept in cages, but in spaces with ample room to move around.

Linda strongly recommends that anyone planning to use a kennel condition the dog by leaving him there for day care a few times to see how he does and if he seems to like the kennel. If the dog has been happy during his stay, he should not have to be dragged in the door the next time he's brought in, she says.

One other point you should be aware of before kenneling your dog: Ask what the policy is on picking up your dog. There have been owners who returned early from vacation on a Sunday only to find the kennel office closed and no one present with the authority to release their dog to them. Linda says that kennel owners often cannot afford to have the office staffed every day of the week, but that kennels should make some provisions to accommodate dog owners. For instance, in the summer, beach property is often rented from Sunday to Sunday, so in the months of July and August Linda keeps her office open on Sundays. Or, if the kennel has some warning that an owner will be returning on a day or at a time the office is usually closed, special arrangements could be made so that the owner can pick up the dog. Just be sure to ask how the kennel handles dog pickup before you leave your pet there.

# CHAPTER 7

# THE POLITE DOG OWNER

**W**hat every dog owner wants to avoid is complaints from the neighbors about his or her dog. Even worse is having the animal control officer show up at your door or getting called before your local animal matters hearing board because you disobeyed animal control laws.

Almost all complaints about dogs can be avoided if their owners make an effort to be considerate of their neighbors.

## Animal Control Laws

The laws vary around the nation, but, generally, their intent is to protect the public from dogs running at large, from the annoyance of barking dogs, and from the health hazards and unpleasant presence of dog waste.

Picking up your dog's stool from community property isn't always enough. Some laws state that grounds for complaint include "unsanitary, dangerous, or offensive conditions," by virtue of the size or number of animals. This means that, even if your dog goes on your own property, the neighbors still have grounds for complaint if they have to look at it and especially if they can smell it or have reason to believe your yard has unsanitary conditions.

The laws usually do not stipulate that a dog has to keep neighbors awake all night barking before a complaint can be lodged. "Audible" noises from a dog within a building or "on adjacent property" that disturbs the "quiet enjoyment" of neighbors may be grounds for complaint in your area.

Since you are never going to let your dog run loose and you will take precautions to see that your dog never gets out accidentally, this is a part of the law that should not concern you.

## How to Keep the Neighbors from Getting Mad

Get off to a good start. Before getting your dog, and assuming that you already are on speaking terms with your immediate neighbors, mention to them your intention to get a dog. Assure them that you will go out of your way to see that the dog never disturbs them. Mention what a good idea it is to have a dog around as a deterrent to crime.

If they didn't react to this announcement with total disgust, make a point to show them the dog a few days after you get him home. If you have a crotchety but not totally unfriendly neighbor next door, invite the neighbor over to see the new dog. The dog might even win the neighbor's affection. Remember that getting a dog can be like having a party; if you include the neighbors, they are less likely to complain.

If you aren't on good terms with your neighbors or have one that reacted really unfavorably to the news of your dog, the best approach might be to keep the dog away from them. They should hardly ever notice that you have a pet.

# Dog Waste

Even the most avid pet lover will become enraged if he steps in a pile of dog waste during a stroll around his neighborhood. More irate is the mother whose toddler falls into a pile while playing in the kiddie yard, or the apartment dweller who opens her door to the strong odor of dog urine because the neighbor's dog wet in the hallway again. Unfortunately, some urban owners with dogs trained to go on newspaper, in a box, or on a patio so seldom clean up after their dogs that the neighbors start getting whiffs.

In row- and town-house complexes, a major problem occurs when owners fail to clean up after their dogs use the tiny backyards. Neighbors trying to enjoy a summer cookout can't smell the barbecue for the odor next door. Other owners let their dogs urinate on grass, shrubbery, and flowers that cost community associations many thousands of dollars to plant and maintain.

These are situations that can turn neighbors against having any dogs in the neighborhood, and these people have reason to gripe. Besides the offensive odor and the damage dog waste can cause, it is unsanitary. Feces attracts bugs and sometimes rodents, and it sometimes contains worms that can be transmitted to children.

Be meticulous about cleaning up after your dog and pressure dog owners who aren't to be more responsible. You should go out of your way to see that your neighbors are never offended by the sight or smell of your dog's waste. On the other hand, it is sometimes appropriate to let your neighbors know that you are making an effort. If, for instance, you live in a row house, ask neighbors from time to time: "You haven't noticed any offensive odor from our yard, have you? I clean up after the dog diligently, but in case there's ever a problem, be sure to let me know."

Sometimes, the problem arises when you are away and there's a sitter caring for your dog who does not clean up; notify neighbors before you leave that there will be a sitter. This way, the neighbor will be more understanding about the temporary mess and can let you know if you are paying someone to do a job they aren't doing.

If you live in an area where there are irresponsible owners and you have a community association newsletter, ask if you can publish a request *from dog owners* asking that everyone with pets be considerate. This will let the neighbors without dogs know that there are people with dogs who are responsible.

**Note:** The penalty for failing to clean up after your dog in New York City or for letting your dog run off his leash ranges from $50 to $100.

## Barking

If your dog barks only when strangers come around, tell your neighbors: "If you ever hear my dog barking, beware — there's someone around who shouldn't be." They may learn to appreciate the dog's presence.

A dog who barks so much that she disturbs neighbors all day while you are at work or who keeps neighbors awake all night won't and should not be tolerated. First, ask your neighbors regularly if they ever hear your dog barking; *ask before you ever have a complaint.* Some owners have dogs who are disturbing neighbors and never even know it, because the dogs do not bark when their owners are home. If you ask a neighbor and find that your dog is making a disturbance, take action immediately as outlined in Chapter 5, then check back regularly with neighbors to make sure the problem has been resolved.

Several trainers have written that, sometimes, neighbors complain that a dog is barking even when she isn't; to resolve this problem, the dog owner must enlist the help of other neighbors to testify that the neighbor complaining is wrong. Another option is to enlist the help of local animal control officers, or a police officer if your community has a community relations division specializing in neighbor disputes. In some instances, an objective outsider with an official presence can solve the problem.

## Lunging and Growling

Neighbors will not appreciate your dog if he lunges and growls at them every time they pass you and your dog on the sidewalk or in the hallway. Apologize for your dog's behavior and, so that the neighbor can hear, tell your dog "No, no!" It helps to tell the dog, "You must never growl at the neighbors!" even though this is for the benefit of the neighbor, not the dog. Keep in mind that dogs often take their owner's lead — if you treat someone like a friend, they will, too. So, when you see a neighbor approaching, talk to the dog in a cheerful, pleasant voice and greet the neighbor that way, too. Your dog might decide to wag his tail instead of lunge.

The alternative is to walk the other way if you see a neighbor coming whom your dog doesn't like and, of course, train your dog to obey you and to heel!

## Visiting with Your Dog

If you haven't successfully trained your dog not to charge the front door and jump up on visitors, leash him in a safe place when you have company in your home or confine him to one section of the house. Some people really are terrified of dogs. Institute training as soon as possible and teach your dog not to charge the front door and jump on guests. It's actually easier than battling the dog or leashing him every time you have company.

If you want to take your dog along when going to someone else's home, especially for overnight visits, be sure that your friends or relatives want the dog to come. You can find out how they feel about it without putting them on the spot by mentioning beforehand that "I should be able to come, but first I have to make arrangements for someone to keep the dog" or "for someone to look in on the dog." If they respond with no more than an "Okay," that means you should not bring the dog. But perhaps they'll say, "By all means, bring your pet!"

You may have friends who are avid dog lovers and tolerant of all dog behavior — you know them well enough to feel confident that they won't be upset if your dog wets in the house or chews a shoe. But, generally, your dog should be housebroken and well trained before you take her with you to someone else's home.

Also consider whether you will have to leave your dog alone in the house during the visit; dogs who behave well when left alone in their own home might not behave in a strange house.

Another consideration is whether your friends or relatives have the kind of household that will be safe for your dog and provide good security. If they don't, it might be better to leave the dog at home with a sitter or in a carefully chosen kennel.

## CHAPTER 8

# THE GROOMED DOG

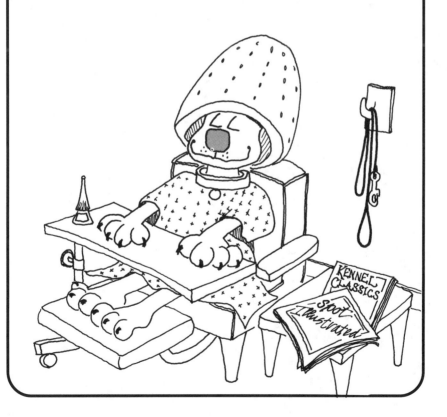

Keeping your dog well groomed will benefit both you and your dog. Occasional full baths and frequent brushing, for instance, will keep your house cleaner and help keep your dog's skin healthy and his coat lustrous. It will also give you the opportunity to check your dog for skin problems. Trimming his nails regularly will keep your wood floors from getting scratched and will prevent the dog's nails from growing so long that they interfere with his stance.

If you are a real zealot for grooming, you can even brush your dog's teeth. Dental care for dogs is now widely recommended to prevent tooth decay and gum disease. It will prevent you from getting a blast of bad dog breath every time your dog's face is near yours and may save you some hefty veterinary bills later on, if you can prevent dog periodontal disease.

Perhaps the greatest advantage of grooming is the rapport it creates between owner and dog. The look in a dog's eyes after you give him this time — time you lavish on him alone with attention and care — will tell you just how special these sessions are for your dog, and it's a rare owner who doesn't find his reaction gratifying.

To make grooming a pleasure for you and the dog, remember these three "G" words as you go about each grooming task:

- Gradual
- Gentle
- Genial

Begin grooming your dog soon after you get him. Gradually introduce him to each grooming task and gently coax him into cooperating. And always be genial — if you approach grooming as a pleasant event, your dog is more likely to view it that way, too.

## Brushing and Combing Your Dog

Because house dogs are subjected to artificial light year-round, they tend to shed continuously, which is why regular brushing is important. To have a healthy skin and coat, you want to remove loose hair and dirt and stimulate your dog's skin, which is what brushing and combing do.

How often you should brush your dog depends on the kind of coat she has. Of course, daily brushing is the ideal for most dogs, but that's an

THE GUILT-FREE DOG OWNER'S GUIDE

unrealistic option for many busy owners. Unless you have a dog with a very elaborate coat, like the Shih Tzu, which really should be brushed daily or most days, a dog with a coat that mats and tangles easily, or a dog with a poor coat, brushing or brushing and combing a few times a week is often adequate.

## Selecting Tools for Brushing Your Dog's Coat

The tools you use to brush your dog must be carefully selected. A dog's skin is more delicate than a human's, and if you don't select the correct tools and use them carefully, you could injure the skin.

If you have a dog with short hair and a smooth coat, such as a boxer or an English bulldog, you may need only one tool, called a *hound glove*, that you put on your hand and rub over the dog's body. Dogs with short, dense coats, such as the dalmatian, or with slightly longer and rough coats, such as the Norfolk terrier, may need brushing and combing. You'll also need to both brush and comb if your dog has very long hair, such as the bearded collie, or an undercoat, such as the Shetland sheep-dog (sheltie), in order to prevent tangling and matting and to control shedding.

Select instruments for grooming that look safe: Combs, for instance, should have rounded teeth, not sharp ones that could puncture your dog's skin. The teeth should be wide enough to go through your dog's coat easily. There are some tools designed just for removing mats, such as the dematting comb, but these do not belong in the hands of unskilled, average dog owners. If your dog's coat is heavily matted or you feel that you need to use tools other than ordinary brushes and combs made for grooming dogs, it would be worth your time and money to take the dog for professional grooming at a grooming parlor recommended by your veterinarian. A dog with a seriously matted coat might also have skin lesions under the mats that need professional attention.

## How to Condition Your Dog to Brushing and Combing

When you brush or comb your dog the first few times, just do a small section and for a short time, to condition her to this procedure. Talk to her in a reassuring and pleasant manner. Your dog will probably think that this is a game, and you may have trouble getting her to stand still; try gently grabbing and holding your dog at the top of one of her back legs, where it runs into the groin area. That will get her attention and help her to stand still long enough for you to brush, so that she can see how good it feels.

If you approach grooming with the three G's in mind — gradual, gentle, and genial — chances are that, each time you try to groom your dog, she'll stand still for longer periods of time. After several sessions, she'll welcome the next one.

## Examine Your Dog While You Groom

While you groom, examine the condition of your dog's skin. Watch for dryness, cuts, lumps or bumps, and parasites. If you find anything other than a minor cut that you can treat with an over-the-counter antiseptic or ointment, or some fleas or ticks that you can remove yourself, contact your veterinarian. Skin tumors particularly or any kind of lesions on your dog's skin should receive prompt attention from the veterinarian.

Don't forget to check the dog's eyes, ears, mouth, feet, and genital area for any signs of abnormality.

## Clipping and Trimming

If you have a breed with a coat that requires occasional trimming or clipping, such as a poodle, or a dog with ears and feet that need trimming, such as a cocker spaniel, go to a professional grooming parlor recommended by your veterinarian. The tools used for clipping and trimming can severely damage your dog's skin if not used correctly. And, as one groomer points out, dogs that jump around while their owner tries to groom them — increasing the risk of injury with a tool — are more likely to stand still for a strange, professional groomer.

Some dogs, particularly some of the terriers, have coats that can be plucked and stripped, but unless you plan to show the dog or want to maintain a show-quality coat, these procedures are seldom necessary for average dogs.

## The Dog Bath

Bathing a dog will remove some of the natural oils from the coat, so it's not something you want to do too often, unless your dog has a skin condition that requires frequent bathing with medicated shampoos. You should get advice from your veterinarian or from a breeder about how often your breed of dog should be bathed. Generally, all dogs benefit from a brushing before bathing and should receive a full bath no more than once a month. If your dog has a tendency toward dry skin, your veterinarian may advise full baths no more than once every two months.

Some dogs with very long coats and some with heavy undercoats should seldom receive a full bath; you can use a dry shampoo recommended by your veterinarian at other times.

## Sponge Bathing

To help keep your dog clean between full baths, use a soft wash cloth and warm water to wipe your dog's face, behind (not in) his ears, under and around his tail, his feet, and anywhere else he's gotten dirty. To avoid spreading germs, don't wipe his feet or his tail area then wipe his face and eyes. Dry him well with a soft towel. How often you need to sponge-bathe the dog depends on how dirty your dog gets and where; he may need only his feet bathed because he gets them dirty during outdoor walks, or he may need his face wiped if he was rooting in dirt outside or if his eyes tend to run, which is common in poodles.

## The Full Bath

If you introduce the full bath to your dog gradually, she may come to love it so much she'll willingly jump into her bathtub. There's a mixed-breed poodle from Pennsylvania that so loves getting wet that the owner has to shut the dog out of the bathroom when bathing to keep the dog from jumping in every day!

Since urban owners usually don't have a basement washtub to use for bathing, you'll probably have to use the bathtub or shower stall.

THE GROOMED DOG

## Equipment for the Full Bath

The most important piece of equipment you'll need is something to keep the dog from slipping in the tub; dogs who feel they have insecure footing will panic, stiffen their legs, and fight frantically to get out. If you have one, use a large rubber bath mat. If you don't have this item or if you have a large dog, use a large wet towel in the bottom of the tub or shower stall. Do not depend on those anti-slip decals that you stick on the floor of your bathtub; they don't cover enough of the tub to prevent the dog from slipping.

Another piece of equipment that will make bathing your dog easier is a spray hose attached to the faucet. If you don't have one, you can rinse the dog with a pitcher, but it will take twice the time and is less likely to get all the soap out.

Consult with your veterinarian about the best kind of shampoo to use on your dog's coat, especially if you need to use a flea shampoo. Because a dog's skin differs from that of a human, the shampoo used on them should be one designed for their skin. And, if your dog's skin is dry, your veterinarian might want you to follow up the bath with a skin conditioner for dogs; some owners find that Alpha-Keri Bath Oil works well.

The last item you'll need is plenty of thick towels on hand to dry the dog immediately after bathing.

---

**TIP**

If you think that your dog might have fleas but aren't sure, use a large, absorbent white towel as your dog's bath mat to help you spot them as they fall off when you rinse the dog.

---

## How to Give the Dog a Full Bath

Before you bathe the dog, run the water, adjust the temperature, and test it on your wrist as you would a baby's bottle, to make sure it's not too cold and especially not too hot, which could burn the dog's skin. While you do this, begin talking to the dog in a tone of voice that communicates gentleness and fun.

Don't fill the tub; dogs are more likely to protest if they have to stand in water or are immersed in it. Put the dog in the tub and, to condition him to the water a bit, spray only his paws.

If your dog panics and starts struggling frantically to get out as soon as you wet his feet, STOP! Keep up the friendly banter as though this was great fun, dry the dog (which often becomes a dog's favorite part of this routine), and call it quits for the day. Then try again a day or two later, gradually conditioning your dog; once he tolerates getting his feet wet, then you can move on to a complete bath.

Begin by wetting the dog's neck, especially if you are bathing to get rid of fleas. If you start at the tail and work up, the fleas will run up the dog's body and hide out on his head. Now wet from the neck down to the tail. Don't forget the insides of his legs and his tummy. After he is wet, apply shampoo and massage well. Then start rinsing. Getting the last bit of soap out is important; if any is left on your dog's skin, it will irritate him.

Do not wash the dog's head and face during a full bath; getting water in the dog's ears is harmful, so it's best to wash these areas with a warm washcloth before or after the full bath (see below). To keep water from running into the ears, try to use one hand (or have someone else lend a hand) to hold up the dog's head during the bath. Some groomers and veterinarians strongly advise that you put cotton in your dog's ears to prevent water from getting in them. The dog's ear canal is more vertical and retains water more easily than a human's, which can lead to an infection.

Dry your dog thoroughly with towels, taking care not to tangle his hair if he has a long coat. Until the dog is completely dry, keep the house warm after you bathe him, and don't let him outside if it's cool or cold, so that he doesn't get chilled. An ideal way to dry a dog with a heavy or long coat is by brushing while using a hand-held blow-dryer set on low heat — use extreme care so as not to burn the dog's skin. You may want to try and condition your dog to sit still for blow-drying, but if the dog really protests, don't force the issue — use towels.

## Grooming Your Dog's Ears

If you need to occasionally wipe out your dog's outer ears because of wax buildup or dirt, use a soft washcloth wrapped around your finger and dipped in mineral oil. Don't reach into the canal and don't use anything else in your dog's ear — including water — unless you are directed to do so by your veterinarian. Contact your veterinarian if your dog seems to have excessive wax buildup, or if the dog's ear contains a brown or black waxlike substance, which could be ear mites. Even urban dogs can contract mites, which require special medication to eradicate and, if not treated promptly, can spread to other parts of the dog's body. Dogs with mites generally will shake or flop their head from side to side, paw at their ears, and scratch.

# Grooming Your Dog's Nails

Dogs that frequently walk or run on hard pavement wear their nails down. Urban dogs, who spend most of their life indoors — often on soft, carpeted floors — don't wear down their nails and so need regular nail clipping. Otherwise, their nails could grow so long that they interfere with the dog's stance.

To tell if your dog's nails are too long, observe her standing on a hard floor. If her nails touch the floor, they are too long. If your dog has *dewclaws* — the nails on the inside of her legs above the feet — they'll need regular trimming to keep them from growing around and into her skin. You can have your veterinarian or a groomer do the clipping, but it really isn't hard to learn, and doing it yourself will save you some money.

Begin grooming your dog's nails soon after you get her; the longer you wait, the less likely she is to cooperate.

If it turns out that you have a struggle on your hands no matter how carefully you try to condition the dog to clipping, or if you are just too nervous to do it without mutilating the dog's nails, have a professional do it for you.

## Tools for Nail Clipping

Buy a nail-clipping tool made specifically for dog nails that has a spring action and a double-sided cutting edge, so you can make a quick, clean cut. Ask a knowledgeable pet store employee to recommend a good clipper of this kind and don't skimp on this tool.

You might also want to buy a file, in case you end up with a rough edge that needs smoothing, and a styptic pencil, in case you accidentally hit a vein.

## How to Clip Nails

The most important point to remember about nail clipping is to avoid clipping the nail vein. Spend some time observing your dog's nails while he is at rest to look for the vein; it's a pinkish core that comes close to the tip of the nail. When you clip, you'll want to clip below the end of that vein.

If your dog's nails have gotten very long, absolutely *do not clip off a large portion to get*

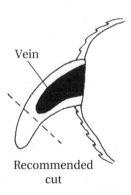

Vein

Recommended cut

*Clip off only a small portion of the nail below the nail vein.*

*them to the desired length.* As the nails grow, so do the veins. As the nails are clipped, the veins recede, so you'll have to take off a tiny bit of nail every several days to get the vein and the nail back to where they should be. This method of clipping a tiny bit off at a time is also the only way to clip black-colored nails, because you can't see the vein in them.

Dogs do not like to have their nails clipped, because clipping exerts pressure that seems to cause an uncomfortable sensation. It's imperative, then, that you gradually condition the dog to clipping if you don't want each session to be a struggle. Start out by playing with your dog's nails to get him used to your handling them. Do that several times. Then start calling the dog to you, lift each paw, and play with his nails. Sweet-talk him and give him a treat. Do that several times.

Next, add the clippers, but don't clip. As you lift a paw, take a nail and put it in the clipper; let the dog get used to the tool, and use the opportunity to observe the place you want to cut.

After you've conducted several of these dry-run sessions — continuing to sweet-talk the dog — and when you think that both you and the dog are ready, try clipping just one nail. File a bit if you've left a rough edge. Give the dog plenty of praise and a treat, and act like this little session was great fun. If your dog is particularly cooperative, continue and do another nail. If the dog tries to take off, which most dogs are likely to do, don't try to force him to cooperate and create a struggle. Just keep up the short sessions and build on them.

Don't, however, let your dog get out of nail clipping too easily. Some dogs will act as though you are hurting them even if you aren't. If you don't hit the vein and draw blood, it's unlikely that you caused pain, because the nerve in the dog's nail is associated with the vein. These dogs also require gradual conditioning to nail clipping, but the owner might have to be a bit firmer about getting them to cooperate.

If you have a dog that has been cooperating with nail clipping but suddenly protests, carefully check his nails and paws for any abnormalities, such as a foreign object embedded in the paw or for a cracked, sore nail. Carefully check for soreness at the point where the nail goes into the paw, which could signal an infection. Any of these abnormalities requires a call to the veterinarian.

### If You Nick a Vein

Don't panic. A nicked nail vein will bleed profusely, and, if you've never seen it, you'll think you've done fatal damage. First, get the dog to be still. The more he runs around, the more the nail will bleed. Use a clean cloth rinsed in cool water to apply direct pressure. The nail should stop bleeding soon if you keep the dog still. You can also apply a styptic pencil. If you really did cut so deep that the nail continues to bleed profusely, even if the dog isn't running around, call the veterinarian.

### How Often to Clip Nails

How often you will have to clip nails depends on how fast your dog's nails grow; in your case, once a month may be adequate. Others may find that trimming the nails every couple of weeks is necessary. It also depends on your level of skill; if you do not feel confident in what you are doing, clip less of each nail at a time but clip more often. If you're pretty good at it and can cut more nail off without hitting the vein, you'll have to clip less often.

## Care of Your Dog's Teeth

Tooth decay can occur in dogs, but the more common problem is gum disease resulting from tartar buildup. Tartar is more likely to accumulate if you live in an area with hard water and if your dog eats mostly soft foods. Some of the small dogs seem to be more prone to tartar buildup and gum disease.

Your dog doesn't have to be old to get gum disease. Dr. Joseph J. Seneczko says he's seen younger dogs with gum disease that was so bad that infection set in and spread into the dog's sinuses, gums, or muzzle.

If your dog has brown stains on his teeth near the gum line, he has tartar. The symptoms of gum disease include bad breath, bleeding from the teeth when the dog chews, and (sometimes) excess salivation.

### How to Prevent Gum Disease

The easiest way to prevent gum disease is to see that your dog's diet includes items that help reduce tartar buildup. Give her crunchy dry dog food instead of a soft dog food if she'll eat it. Give her hard dog biscuits and nylon bones to chew daily.

More and more dog owners have started brushing their dogs' teeth, but you've got to initiate brushing while the dog is still young; otherwise she isn't likely to tolerate the procedure. You can use toothpaste especially designed for dogs or baking soda moistened with water. Gradually condition your dog if you brush her teeth — start by just rubbing a moistened cloth over one tooth, then add the cleansing agent, and gradually build up to brushing all the teeth. Be sure to rinse off the cleansing agent well.

Have your veterinarian regularly check your dog's teeth in case they need professional cleaning.

## CHAPTER 9

# THE
# FIT DOG

*Exercising and Feeding Confined Dogs*

For most owners, exercising their dogs does a lot more than simply keep their pets healthy. As you've read throughout this book, it can also prevent dogs from developing destructive behavior problems. There are, however, substantial health benefits for your dog, including the prevention of obesity, which can lead to heart disease. A dog who gets regular exercise is more likely to have healthy skin and a nice coat than a dog who doesn't get much exercise.

Certainly, getting the dog outside regularly for walks and jogging sessions is best and, for almost all dogs except some of the toy breeds, it is essential. But on days when this isn't practical or possible, an alternative that many owners fail to consider is indoor exercise. Although most owners play indoors with their dogs, they don't consider expanding the activity to a level that really exercises the dog. Even in the smallest of homes, there's usually at least one room or a hallway that can be used for some romping. Keep in mind, too, that dogs generally will not exercise themselves; they need encouragement from their owners.

As important as exercise is your dog's diet if you want him to be in top shape. Selecting the right food can also make cleaning up after your dog easier.

## How Much Exercise Does a Dog Need?

Consider your dog's breed, size, age, physical condition, and energy level. Obviously, a two-year-old golden retriever is going to need more exercise than a ten-year-old Pekingese. Puppies need lots of activity, but because they are growing rapidly, exercise sessions must be short and gentle; exercise that is too vigorous can damage their musculoskeletal system, especially if they are one of the giant breeds. If your dog is fat, he needs more exercise than he's been getting.

Perhaps the best way to determine how much exercise your dog needs is by his energy level and tolerance for exercise. Dogs who are very active indoors or who demonstrate symptoms of excess energy, such as chewing and barking, need more exercise than they are getting. If a dog walked for 15 minutes isn't even panting and is into everything in the house as soon as you return from your walk, he needs longer walks or supplemental indoor exercise.

But dogs, like humans, must be conditioned to exercise. They need to begin with regular, gentle doses of activity, and their tolerance for exercise must be increased gradually. Vigorous exercise sessions should be preceded by walking to warm up the muscles.

More and more trainers are warning about the perils of the "weekend dog athlete"; dogs who remain relatively motionless all week and then receive vigorous activity on the weekends can easily injure themselves. Dogs who are allowed to play Frisbee or other games in which they jump into the air only on occasion may be more prone to developing hip dysplasia.

With any kind of activity, you must take care not to work the dog so hard that it takes him an inordinate amount of time for his breathing to return to normal. You want him just panting, but not so overworked that he flops down on the floor in exhaustion.

Dr. Joseph J. Seneczko cautions that, during the times you give your dog vigorous exercise, such as a jog around the park, be sure to give the dog biscuits periodically throughout the workout — the dog will need extra energy — and to provide water often.

## Indoor Exercise

Here are some ideas for indoor activities you can participate in with your dog, which will help keep him in shape and dispel excess energy. Select the ones that you think you would enjoy doing with your dog and then do them enough so that you can see that the dog is getting a workout. One word of caution: Don't let your dog race around on slippery floors inside the house, because he could fall. Use a carpeted room, or select an activity safe for the kind of floor surface you have.

### Fetch and Catch

Most dogs love to fetch, although you've got to teach them how. Just about any lightweight dog toy will do; a doggie "newspaper" made of rubber is a favorite fetching toy, because the shape is easy for the dog to pick up. Just throw the object; most dogs will go for it. Then call them back to you and reward them with vocal praise and some pats on the head.

A variation of this game is playing kick-ball fetch. Play with your shoes off and keep your foot on the floor, gently pushing a ball away from you so that you don't kick the dog in the face. Use a ball small enough for the dog to pick up and return to you.

To play catch, select a ball that is lightweight. The ball must not be so small that it could lodge in the dog's throat on impact, and not so big that the dog can't catch it in his mouth. Racquetballs are a good size for some of the larger to medium-sized dogs. Toss the ball into the air, but not too high, and see if your dog tries to catch it. Dogs interested in this game can become excellent catchers. Teach them to bring the ball back to you.

> **TIP**
> To save money on your dog toys, look in the phone book under "Pet Supplies" to see if you can find stores that offer products to the public at wholesale or discount prices. Another possible source is schools for dog training, which sometimes have a sideline business selling dog products at a discount. You can save a lot!

## Beach Ball

If you've got a spacious room or hall in your home and don't have a lot of breakables around, an inexpensive beach ball can provide hours of fun for your dog, especially if she learns to bat and push it around the house with her nose and paws. The fun in it for the dog seems to be trying to manipulate the ball. Try the standard, giant-sized beach ball for large dogs; there are smaller beach balls that can be used for small dogs. Most dogs can pop beach balls with their teeth, though, then tear and eat the plastic, so this toy should be used only with your supervision and put away at other times.

## "Obedience" Play

When you have taught your dog the commands for sit, down, come, and heel, the commands can be used for indoor play and exercise sessions either alone or combined with other games. As you have the dog sit, lie down, and sit again, he is working his muscles.

Play "hide-and-seek" by having your dog stay, then going to another room and calling the dog. Change from room to room. Or have the dog heel and march around the house off-leash, practicing stops and turns. Have him accompany you, going through the commands, as you do chores. If you have to go to another floor in your apartment building to do the laundry or out front to get the mail, put the dog on a leash and take him with you, using the appropriate commands.

Some of this may sound ridiculous, but it gets the dog moving, and, if you approach the sessions excitedly and give the dog lots of praise, it reinforces obedience training. Obedience play is also a way of providing activity for dogs that aren't interested in playing other games.

### Aerobics

If you're an exercise-conscious person and work out in your home, perhaps using aerobics tapes, encourage your dog to participate. If you usually run in place, run instead around the house, encouraging the dog to follow; if she's the exuberant type, she'll catch right on and run around with you.

## Outdoor Exercise

Taking your dog outside for walks or jogs not only exercises him, it socializes him as well and can make him a more adaptable pet. It also helps keep his nails worn down.

Have your dog sit each time you stop to chat with a neighbor or are waiting to cross a street, if the pavement's not too hot. The sitting maneuver works the muscles and keeps dogs out of the way of others.

Dogs taken for walks over the same stretch day after day become bored; you should vary where you walk whenever possible and talk to your dog. But watch where you walk; avoid taking the dog through broken glass, on walks with tiny pebbles that might harm his paws, or on scorching hot pavement.

Even if you've got a large park nearby with an area away from traffic, *absolutely do not take your dog off his leash outside* unless he's in a fenced-in area, even if he's considered well trained. One loud, unfamiliar noise or a strange animal might be all it takes to prompt your dog to take off into traffic before you can catch him. Instead, try teaching your dog to run circles around you, so long as the leash gives him some freedom of movement. (Make sure your area doesn't have a law making six feet the maximum leash length permitted.)

Try to find a fenced-in area, such as a neighbor's or friend's yard where you can let your dog romp safely without his leash at least once weekly. Good off-leash games for outdoor fenced-in areas are fetch and catch, chasing beach balls, or soccer. There are soccer-type balls made especially for dogs. The Kong toys, which bounce in a different direction every time they're thrown, are good toys for playing in the grass.

For outdoor fetch, don't use tree limbs or sticks; they can injure a dog's mouth. Use the same kind of soft fetch toy you would use indoors. And try to find a playmate for your dog — another dog that gets along well with yours — to romp with outdoors.

If your dog is in good physical condition, regularly gets lots of exercise, and your veterinarian thinks that jumping off the ground is safe for him, Frisbee is a popular game with dogs. In some urban areas, there are even Frisbee competitions for dogs.

An outdoor activity to avoid is bicycling with dogs; it's too easy for them to get their paws run over or caught in a spoke, and it's too easy to overwork them.

## Feeding Your Dog

Don't forget the water. Dogs need water even more than they need food, and your dog should have a sturdy bowl that can't be tipped over. Refill it several times daily and clean it often.

Among the commercial foods available are dry foods, canned foods, and semi-moist foods. Dry foods usually are cheaper than the others, and they help keep your dog's teeth and gums in good condition.

### Which Dog Food?

Your primary concern should be nutritional adequacy. Dogs have nutritional needs that are different from humans', and that's why they should have a food designed especially for them. You may have gotten your dog from a breeder who recommends cooking for your dog; the recipes vary, but might include minced meat or raw liver mixed with other ingredients. But chances are that a commercial dog food is more likely to consistently give your dog what he needs than a homemade concoction. Busy dog owners also need to keep it simple — don't make feeding your dog unnecessarily complicated.

If, however, you are going to be changing the dog's diet from what he was getting before you got him, do it gradually by slowly replacing the old food with the new so that you don't upset the dog's digestive system.

Generally, your dog should do fine with any of the name-brand, commercially available dog foods that are labeled "100 percent complete and balanced nutrition." Always check with your veterinarian to make sure you are choosing a nutritious dog food and, unless you have a huge dog, don't buy large quantities of dog food and store it — it will lose some of its nutritional value sitting on the shelf.

THE GUILT-FREE DOG OWNER'S GUIDE

Urban owners need to consider the stool a particular food will produce if they are going to be scooping up after their dogs. Concentrated dry foods produce a drier, more compact stool that's easy to pick up; they initially cost more than unconcentrated dry foods, but the supply lasts longer because you feed less to the dog each meal. Some fine foods that you might want to try include Hill's Science Diet, Iams, or Purina's Pro Plan. These foods are not sold in grocery stores; you must buy them from the veterinarian or in a pet supply store, which makes them inconvenient for some owners to purchase. However, Purina now has in grocery stores a product called O.N.E., which is concentrated.

---

**TIP**

Puppies will find it easier to eat their meals off of a flat, heavy plate that won't slide around. As they get older, you can buy a regular dog bowl. If you have a dog with long ears, such as a cocker spaniel, you will want to get a bowl designed to keep their ears out of the food.

---

If cleaning up after your dog isn't a major concern and you don't need a concentrated food, consider trying Purina's Hi-Pro, a dry food that is available in grocery stores.

### Should I Give the Dog Vitamins?

You are more likely than not to read that, if your dog is apparently healthy and on a sound dog food, vitamins are unnecessary. It's also true that some vitamins are toxic if given in high enough doses, or if they are used when the dog is already on a food with vitamin supplements in it.

However, if your dog's coat is dull or her skin is dry and itchy, if you think your dog is under stress for any reason, or if your dog eats grass and sticks or weird things like peeling plaster off the walls, ask your veterinarian about prescribing vitamins. Some trainers have found that improving a dog's diet or correcting a dietary deficiency may eliminate chewing problems.

### Special Needs

Puppies need more nutrients than older dogs because they are growing rapidly, so use one of the name-brand commercial foods that are designed especially for them. Be sure to check them out beforehand with your veterinarian.

You may find that the food you choose doesn't agree with your dog. For instance, one dog might be intolerant of all canned food and throw up after eating. Some dogs won't eat dry food unless it's mixed with a little canned food or with some hot water or chicken broth; others love the crunchy texture of dry food alone. Individual variations in tolerance and preference for certain foods isn't unusual, and you may have to experiment a bit to find the best diet for your dog.

For older urban dogs, who get a minimum of outdoor exercise and are overweight, there are reduced-calorie brand name foods available. If your dog is already tipping the scales, you could reduce the amount of food that you are giving the dog; check with your veterinarian first. If the dog's hunger is not satisfied, try adding some cooked rice to help fill the stomach. But Dr. Seneczko points out that rice will add bulk to the stool, as will some of the low-cal foods when compared to a dry concentrated food. That means you could end up with a stool that is messy to clean up. An alternative to changing the diet is to increase the dog's activity level.

If your dog has a chronic illness, such as kidney or heart disease, your veterinarian may recommend a special diet for your dog.

---

**TIP**

Consider using small bits of firm vegetables or fruit — the end of the broccoli you usually toss, an apple slice, or a crunchy carrot. These are low-cal snacks, and, since you usually have these foods in the house anyway, you can save money on commercial dog treats. They should be used sparingly until you are certain they agree with your dog's digestive system. As in humans, apples particularly may help keep a dog's breath fresh.

---

## How Often to Feed the Dog

Weaned puppies need to eat four meals a day up until the age of about 12 weeks. For busy owners who can't be there to meet this schedule, leave out a bowl of food so that the dog can "free-feed." Don't use food that can spoil — dry food is best. An alternative is to ask a reliable neighbor to help out with a couple of the feedings during these several crucial weeks when the dog needs several meals daily.

After 12 weeks, you can reduce the number of meals to about three daily, or free-feed, and, after six months of age, you can feed the dog twice daily. At one year of age, one meal a day is okay, but more trainers now seem to recommend that isolated house dogs get two meals; they are more likely to be calmer and to sleep instead of chew if they have a full tummy when they are left alone.

Owners of large dogs who eat huge amounts of food also should break up the dog's meal into two smaller feedings; these dogs are susceptible to a condition called *bloat* or *overeating syndrome*. It is characterized by a buildup of gas and fluid in the stomach, which causes considerable distress to the dog and can evolve into a life-threatening situation if the stomach actually twists. It seems to occur more often in large male dogs, and especially when the dogs are exercised within an hour or two after eating.

---

**TIP**
Puppies who are weaned do not need milk. In fact, they might be intolerant of it and wind up with a case of diarrhea.

---

When deciding on a feeding time, urban owners need to think about the time the dog is going to have to defecate as a result of feeding. What goes in comes out about 8 to 12 hours later — puppies defecate sooner after eating than larger dogs. But bowel activity differs among dogs, and you might have to do a little experimenting, especially if you will be taking your dog outside to go. Vary the schedule gradually — by half-hour increments — to get the results you want.

### Treats and What a Dog Should Not Eat

Dogs should not eat so much scrap human food or dog treats that they spoil their appetites for their regular full meals of dog food, which they need for adequate nutrition. If you give your dog a treat every other minute, it could contribute to obesity and have the dog begging all the time.

If you are having trouble getting the dog on a schedule that has her defecating at a convenient time for you, perhaps it's the treats coming through.

If your dog is becoming overweight, use small treats sparingly and use low-cal treats. Just because you have a medium-sized dog, you don't have to give her dog treats for medium-sized dogs; a smaller biscuit for a tiny dog is fine. Biscuits are good because they help keep your dog's teeth clean.

## Dogs That Eat Strange Things

Some dogs have a craving to eat dirt and other foreign matter. This condition is called *pica*. It can signal a nutritional deficiency in your dog and requires a consultation with your veterinarian.

THE FIT DOG

Much to their horror, some dog owners find that their dogs have eaten their own stool, which is called *coprophagy.* Why dogs do this isn't really understood, but you should know that it isn't that uncommon. If your veterinarian thinks the dog is healthy and his diet adequate, the cause of the problem could be the way the dog was handled before you had him. If he came from a pet shop or puppy mill where he was not fed well and where his cage wasn't cleaned often, he may have gotten into the habit of eating his own stool because he was hungry. The only solution is to pick up the stool as soon as the dog defecates so he can't get to it. It's usually puppies who demonstrate this behavior, which they usually outgrow.

Some dogs love eating grass. Why they do this isn't known for certain. You may hear that they need more fiber in their diet, or that they are using grass as an *emetic* — to make themselves vomit — because they have an upset stomach. If your dog is in good health and eats grass, and if the grass hasn't been treated with chemicals, it's probably not a threat to your dog's health. However, when dogs who eat grass defecate, the grass may remain in strings and come out only halfway, causing the dog to drag his rear end on the ground to dislodge the grass. This can create quite a mess for the urban dog owner caught without tissues to clean the dog — and that's reason enough not to let your dog eat grass!

# CHAPTER 10

# THE
# DOCTORED DOG

*Health Care Needs and Problems*

T he first task relating to your dog's health care is finding a veterinarian. Take your dog to one the first day or two after you get him for an examination and to discuss his health care needs, such as diet, exercise, and protection against infectious diseases.

Immunization is just as important for urban dogs as it is for dogs living in the country. Rabies, for instance, has not been eliminated by urbanization. In fact, in the Washington, D.C., metropolitan area, the disease has become a significant problem among raccoons, who continue to inhabit those areas of woodland that remain despite heavy development. The presence of rabies or any other infectious, deadly disease puts pets at risk, and the only way to protect them is by immunization. Immunization of domestic dogs against rabies is also required by law to protect the human population.

Although the other health care needs of dogs are similar no matter where they live, there are problems that you might be more likely to encounter if your dog is a house pet. Obesity, for instance, may be more likely to occur in a confined and inactive dog. House dogs left alone a lot become bored, and they may be more likely to develop lick sores. Because they are exposed to so much artificial heat, a dry skin and coat might become a problem.

## Finding a Veterinarian

Ask friends and neighbors for recommendations. Another good source is your local humane society. Certainly try to find a veterinarian who's close to home for convenience and so that you can get your dog help quickly in case of an emergency.

On your first visit, notice whether the veterinarian and staff seem polite, efficient, and especially caring and kind toward the animals. Is the place clean, and does the examination given to your dog seem methodical and thorough? If not, you probably won't want to use that veterinary clinic again.

Your questions about the care of the dog and about the charges for services should be answered patiently and completely, no matter how mundane they appear to be.

Ask about emergency services. The veterinarian or his or her staff should provide you with the name, phone number, and address of an emergency clinic to use at times the veterinarian's office isn't open. This information, along with the phone number and address of the veterinarian, should be permanently posted by your telephone at home.

## Vital Vaccines

Infectious diseases in dogs can be contracted in a variety of ways, depending on the disease; some can be transmitted just by contact among animals, and others require exposure to the urine or feces of an infected dog. For many of the diseases listed in this section, prevention is the only option; if a dog contracts one of these diseases, the chances of a cure may be slim. That's why it is so important to avoid any delays in getting your dog immunized, and why you must not take a dog outside until your veterinarian has given you the okay to do so (and given your dog the necessary shots).

Below are listed some of the major diseases your dog should be immunized against regularly. They are all viral diseases with the exception of leptospirosis, which is a bacterial disease. The symptoms for many of these diseases are similar and range from vomiting and diarrhea to convulsions.

**Distemper** — occurs primarily in puppies and affects several of the dog's systems, including the nervous and respiratory systems.

**Hepatitis** — primarily affects the liver.

**Leptospirosis** — primarily affects the kidneys.

**Parainfluenza** — affects the respiratory system.

**Parvovirus** — attacks throughout the body, including the gastrointestinal system and the heart.

**Rabies** — attacks the nervous system.

If you buy a puppy, he should have received some of these vaccinations already, especially the one for distemper. No matter what the age of your new dog, ask the seller for the immunization records and take copies to your veterinarian. Subsequent shots will be needed during puppyhood and then annually. Your dog probably will receive the

DHLPP, which stands for distemper, hepatitis, leptospirosis, parainfluenza, and parvovirus. The rabies vaccine is administered separately, and your veterinarian may use a vaccine that is given annually or every three years after the initial shots.

## Worms

The most common kinds of worms are intestinal parasites and include hookworms, roundworms, tapeworms, and whipworms. Dogs may have worms when they are born or acquire them through contact with feces from infected dogs. Depending on the type of worm the dog has, the symptoms vary and include diarrhea and vomiting, anemia, and, in puppies, impaired growth.

Regularly take a sample of your dog's stool to the veterinarian, who can check for the presence of worms and treat the dog if necessary.

Another kind of worm that is a serious threat to dogs is heartworm; just as the name implies, it lives in the dog's heart. Because it is transmitted by mosquitoes, dogs can contract this type of worm easily. Fortunately, there is a simple preventive treatment available, which you should discuss with your veterinarian. During warm-weather months, when mosquitoes are around, you may be instructed to give your dog a pill daily; there is also a once-a-month pill now available. To prevent serious infection with this potentially fatal disease, it is imperative that you follow your veterinarian's instructions about how to give the treatment. He or she will also want to regularly test your dog for heartworm, which requires drawing blood.

## The Tail-Docking and Ear-Cropping Controversy

If your dog is of a breed that customarily has the tail *docked,* or cut off, the deed probably has been done before you got the dog, since docking is performed soon after birth. Some of the breeds that usually have a docked tail are the Airedale terrier, the Norfolk and Norwich terriers, the cocker spaniels, the weimaraner, the boxer, the giant schnauzer, and the miniature and standard poodles.

Ear cropping, once widely practiced on several breeds, including the Doberman pinscher and the Great Dane, is no longer permitted in the United Kingdom. Although it has been rumored that some states in the United States have outlawed ear cropping, this is not the case as of this writing, according to Guy Hodge, director of data and information for the Humane Society of the United States. Some states have, however, passed laws making it illegal for anyone other than a veterinarian to crop ears, a procedure sometimes performed by breeders and trainers.

Cropping is required to show some dogs.

To crop the ears, the dog is given anesthesia, and the outer flap of the ear is cut off and stitched into a shape that eventually should make the ears stand up. The ears have to be taped up and cared for for several weeks.

You may be told by cropping advocates that ear cropping doesn't bother the dog. But if you have ever had stitches, you can imagine how badly it can hurt and itch to have a wound around the entire edge of your ears and stitches in them. This author can tell you from experience that cropping is not necessarily painless for dogs; some of them will whimper in distress for days after the procedure, pawing at their ears.

Because the purpose of both tail docking and ear cropping is strictly cosmetic, neither should be performed, in Mr. Hodge's opinion.

For average owners with family pets, there seems to be no reason to have a dog's ears cropped, and if you do have visions of showing your dog and live in a place where cropping is required to show your breed, carefully consider whether a few moments in the show ring is really worth the expense of ear cropping and the risk of making your dog unnecessarily miserable. If enough people would refuse to have their dogs' ears cropped and forgo the show ring, the practice would have to stop; tail docking might also be abandoned.

**TIP**

If you want to become really well informed about the home medical care of dogs, including emergency care, get a copy of a book called *The Dog Owner's Home Veterinary Handbook,* by Delbert G. Carlson, D.V.M., and James M. Giffin, M.D., published by Howell Book House.

You may hear from some breeders that cropping reduces the incidence of ear infections, and while there may be some truth to that, it's still not a good reason to have your dog's ears cropped. Robert W. Kirk, Professor of Medicine Emeritus, New York State College of Veterinary Medicine, Cornell University, and a past president of the American College of Veterinary Dermatology, says that it is true that breeds with floppy ears may have a higher incidence of ear infections. But so might dogs with naturally erect ears that have hair in them. Anything that reduces air flow in the ear may increase the risk of infection. All that means is that owners of dogs with floppy ears or erect ears with hair in them should be on the lookout for ear problems.

If for some reason you are bound and determined to have your dog's ears cropped, be sure to have it done by a veterinarian who has had considerable experience cropping ears for your particular breed of dog, since the procedure requires aesthetic as well as surgical skill.

# Spaying and Castration

If you are like most dog owners, you probably have no intention of breeding your dog, so spaying your female or castrating your male dog — which is permanent surgical sterilization — is something you'll probably want to have done. There are birth control drugs for female dogs, but, for average owners, it seems more practical to permanently prevent pregnancy than to have to fool with medication throughout the dog's reproductive years.

Neutered dogs are generally considered easier to keep. In females, neutering eliminates the "heat" period, which can be messy in a confined environment and attract stray males to your home. It's a well-accepted fact that neutered male dogs are more likely to be content sticking close to home than unneutered males. In both sexes, neutering reduces the incidence of certain diseases associated with the reproductive organs.

You'll hear some dog owners say they want to let their dog have a litter because it will be a good experience for the children. That may be true for some families, but chances are that the children's interest will wane fast and that the parents will be saddled with the responsibility of caring for the puppies and for finding them homes. If you want your kids to have a back-to-nature experience that will teach them something about the birds and the bees, take them to a farm instead.

Don't forget that there already are far more dogs in the world than the human population can properly care for. Why bring more into the world?

### Are There Risks to the Surgery?

Certainly there is some risk in having dogs neutered, because they must be given anesthesia, but, if your dog is generally healthy and you have an experienced, well-qualified veterinarian perform the procedure, it's unlikely you'll encounter complications. Neutering will require careful home care — your dog will be a post-operative patient for a week or two — but it will save you a lot of trouble down the road.

You'll also have to carefully follow your veterinarian's preoperative instructions, which will include the withholding of food and water beginning the night before surgery; this will help prevent potentially deadly *aspiration* — when the stomach's contents are vomited and sucked into the lungs during anesthesia.

Some dog owners swear that neutering made their dogs get fat, but this problem can be controlled simply by reducing the quantity of food given and by increasing activity.

### At What Age Should the Dog Be Neutered?

It used to be said that females should not be spayed until they had experienced one "heat" period, but fewer veterinarians believe that waiting this long is necessary. Many female dogs can be spayed around six months of age or soon thereafter. Males can be castrated closer to the age of one year, and the procedure should be done after puberty, so that it doesn't interfere with their bone development. Check with your veterinarian, because the best time for neutering may vary among different breeds.

## Everyday Health Care Problems

There are a variety of everyday health problems that you are likely to encounter; some may require a call to the veterinarian, but many do not. And many of the items you'll need to care for your dog are likely to be in your medicine cabinet already.

### Minor Cuts and Scrapes

If in a place other than the eye or the ear canal, clean them with peroxide and apply some over-the-counter Neosporin ointment to prevent infection. Bleeding from minor wounds can be stopped with direct pressure with a clean cloth before the wounds are cleaned and treated.

Call the veterinarian for any scrape or injury to the eye, if any wound looks red or has any discharge, which indicates that an infection is setting in, or if your dog has a wound that you think might have been inflicted by another animal.

### Anal Sacs

All dogs have anal sacs, which you may have heard referred to as "scent glands." They are located around the anus. In most dogs, they never require care, but in some dogs, especially small dogs, they tend to block up and may overproduce secretions that cause an unpleasant odor. Many dog owners learn to *express* — apply pressure to — the sacs with guidance from their veterinarian if their dog develops chronic anal sac blockage. Anal sac infection, however, requires treatment from your veterinarian.

## Obesity

Throughout this book, you will see references to the harmful effects of obesity, which include heart disease and diabetes. You can tell if your dog is too fat by checking the skin over his ribs. If you have a short-coated dog, you should be able to see a hint of his ribs; if you have a long-coated dog, you should be able to feel his ribs beneath the skin. If you can't, the dog is too fat. Talk to your veterinarian about how you can reduce or change the dog's diet in a way that will still ensure that he gets enough nutrients, and increase the dog's activity level. In some cases, obesity may be due to a thyroid problem.

## Parasites

Fleas and ticks aren't just a nuisance — they can make your dog sick by transmitting diseases. Fleas can give your dog tapeworm, and some dogs are allergic to fleas and will develop dermatitis if they have fleas. Ticks can transmit serious infectious diseases to dogs and are responsible for the potentially deadly Rocky Mountain spotted fever in humans. Although house dogs probably are less likely to get fleas and ticks than dogs that live outdoors, they are not immune. Fleas might be contracted if your dog has contact with an infected dog, or she might pick some up after a roll in the grass or in fall leaves. Ticks are more commonly found in tall grass and weeds. If your dog scratches, check for fleas, even if you think it's an unlikely possibility. Ticks may not be apparent, so you should feel for them as you pet and groom your dog.

### How to Eradicate Fleas

If you are fairly certain that your dog has been flea-free but you find that she picked one or two up during a trip to the country or during a play session in the park, handpicking the fleas off immediately may be adequate.

If your dog has a bad infestation or if she keeps getting fleas even after you de-flea her, you have to consider the possibility that you've got fleas in the house, which will have to be exterminated by you or a professional. Be sure to read the section on the safe use of pesticides in Chapter 4. A bath in flea shampoo or a dip at the veterinarian's may be in order for the dog while the house is being exterminated, but until you can get the dog in for treatment, pick off fleas to give the dog some relief.

If fleas are proving to be a constant problem, ask your veterinarian about the products available that you can use on your dog to keep fleas off; while flea collars may work adequately, they may irritate the skin of some dogs. There are also flea powders, as well as prescription prod-

THE GUILT-FREE DOG OWNER'S GUIDE

ucts. Use only one flea product at a time to avoid overdosing the dog with pesticides, and check with your veterinarian before using any flea product on puppies — they are more susceptible to toxic substances than adult dogs.

### How to Catch a Flea

This can be tough! They move fast. Some owners soak a cotton ball with alcohol and, when they see a flea, dab it. The alcohol seems to stun the creature, if only for a moment, so that you can nab it between your index finger and thumb. Once you grab it, absolutely do not release the tight pressure between your fingers, or it will jump away.

Keep a tall glass or deep bowl next to you filled about halfway with water while you are picking off fleas. As soon as you grab one, sink your fingers to the bottom of the water and release. (If you fill the bowl or glass to the top with water, these parasites might jump out on you!) Now take the container of water to the bathroom and pour it into the toilet as you are flushing so that the flea can't jump out.

### How to Remove and Eradicate Ticks

These bloodsuckers seem to gravitate toward the dog's ears or crevices in the dog's feet. You might catch one taking a stroll from your dog's foot up to his head. If your dog has been heavily infested, call the veterinarian to see if a dip is indicated. More likely, you need only to pick ticks off.

Ticks that have taken hold used to be removed by first soaking them with alcohol or clear fingernail polish, which was thought to make them open their mouths so that they could be pulled out without leaving their heads in the skin. Burning them off with the tip of a hot match was another favorite old-time method of removal. More recently, it has been said that applying chemicals or heat to ticks only makes them regurgitate into the dog's skin, which might increase the risk of infection.

**TIP**
Use a household flashlight to make it easier to spot fleas on a dog. As you slowly brush the coat against the grain with one hand to expose the skin, shine the light. Fleas usually hang out around a dog's tail, but they will run and hide anywhere they can as you search for them, so you must systematically examine all parts of the dog from tail to head, including inside the legs and around the ears and face. Besides looking for fleas, watch for white and black spots — flea eggs and flea feces — which also indicate that your dog is infested.

The currently recommended method of removal, then, is to remove ticks with tweezers or with your fingers, protected with a tissue. Grab them firmly as near the head as possible and pull. Soak the area of the bite well with peroxide.

If the head remains in the skin, the area probably will dry up in a couple days, and you can scrape the head off and treat the area again with an antiseptic. Occasionally, the site might become infected, in which case you should call the veterinarian for guidance.

Don't forget to wash your own hands well after removing ticks from your dog!

## Skin Problems

Dr. Kirk estimates that, in an average urban veterinary practice, between 20 and 25 percent of the cases involve skin problems. Fleas and flea dermatitis are by far the most common cause of skin problems in dogs. Another common problem is *seborrhea*, an oily, scaly skin condition, which can be controlled with proper treatment.

Nonspecific dry skin — dry skin without any obvious physical or external cause — is another common problem among house dogs. The dog has dry, flaky skin that itches and a dull coat. This condition is more common among urban dogs that are house pets, because they live in artificially heated areas with low humidity; this tends to dry out the skin, just as similar conditions can in humans.

If your dog has dry skin and a dull coat, first see your veterinarian, who can categorize your dog's coat and skin type. It could be that your dog belongs to a breed whose coat is supposed to be coarse and harsh and that there's really no problem. According to Dr. Kirk, average owners should not expect their dogs to always look like show dogs.

If your veterinarian thinks that the dog's coat and skin are abnormally dry for the breed, he or she will review the possible causes. Some dogs need far more fat in their diet than they may be getting. Another potential cause of dry skin is overbathing; owners of house dogs tend to be more fastidious about grooming, because their dogs live in close proximity to them. But overbathing dries out the skin.

Brushing your dog more often may help; it stimulates the skin and increases oil production, which may relieve dryness, Dr. Kirk says.

Some dogs, particularly bored dogs, develop a condition called *lick sores*. They lick and lick one or two specific spots, until the hair is gone and the skin is irritated. Dogs with lick sores generally need far more activity than they are getting. Calluses, thickened areas of skin, might develop from lying on a hard floor; provide padding for the dog.

## Allergies

Dogs can develop allergies, which are another possible cause of skin problems. There are several types of allergies: One develops due to contact with an irritating substance and appropriately is called *contact dermatitis*. In this case, the dog may develop red itchy bumps, hives, or a rash.

*Flea dermatitis*, mentioned in the section on fleas above, can cause similar symptoms, which tend to be found near the dog's hindquarters.

Some dogs develop *food allergies*, which may be indicated by vomiting within a few hours after eating.

Other dogs develop *inhalant allergies*. The major symptom is repeated scratching, often in the facial area and under the legs. The dog may also bite and lick his paws and forelegs or rub his face on the furniture. Some dogs sneeze and have watery eyes, just as humans with hay fever do. You might find areas of hair rubbed off and brown patches, which are pigment changes.

Dogs can be treated for allergies. If the problem is a contact allergy, your veterinarian can prescribe medication to relieve the symptoms and help you pinpoint the cause. Food allergies require a change in diet. Inhalant allergies might be relieved by antihistamines, but generally these do not work as well in dogs as in humans. Dr. Joseph J. Seneczko explains that, in humans, histamine release is often a major factor in the allergic response, but it isn't in dogs, which is why antihistamines may not help much. But dogs can be desensitized to allergies; in fact, symptoms can be reduced or eliminated in about 75 percent of cases with proper treatment. So, if your dog has frequent inhalant allergy symptoms, it may well be worth a trip to the veterinary allergist.

If your dog is allergic, there may be times that he requires steroids, which are anti-inflammatory drugs, to relieve symptoms. Steroids are powerful drugs with potentially serious side effects — they can suppress the body's immune system when used incorrectly — and some dog owners object to their use. However, for the dog with severe scratching and other allergy-associated symptoms, such as hair loss and dermatitis, steroids can provide effective relief. Just be sure to follow your veterinarian's instructions carefully; these drugs have to be tapered off gradually.

## Vomiting and Diarrhea

A dog that gobbles food down, then throws it back up, probably just ate too fast. Healthy puppies seem to throw up a lot more than healthy older dogs. If your dog throws up and there is something like grass or the kid's crayons in the vomitus, you can bet these foreign objects prompted the vomiting. Generally a dog that vomits once and has no other associated symptoms, such as lethargy, loss of appetite, or diarrhea, does not need a trip to the veterinarian.

If your dog vomits more than once, however, or has any other symptoms, even if it's only a subtle change in behavior, certainly call your veterinarian for guidance. A dog who vomits only once, but whose vomitus contains blood — either bright red fresh blood or the characteristic brown flecks of old blood — should be taken immediately to the veterinarian to be checked.

The same holds true for diarrhea. If your dog has one loose stool, which could be caused by an upset in the digestive system due to something she ate or even to an emotional upset, and if she has no other associated symptoms and no signs of blood in the stool, you can probably forgo a call to the veterinarian. But more than one loose stool, a loose stool in a dog with other symptoms, or a stool — firm or loose — that has fresh or dried blood in it means that you should call your veterinarian immediately.

Since dogs can't talk, it is sometimes difficult to determine when they are ill if the signs or symptoms aren't obvious. One way that you can learn to differentiate the normal from the abnormal is to observe your dog's behavior and study her physical appearance when you know she's healthy and in good shape.

Notice the color, shape, and form of your dog's stool. Study her ears, skin, gums, and paws.

## Symptoms of an Ill Dog

Different illnesses often have similar symptoms, and it takes the skills of a veterinarian to make a proper diagnosis. If your dog demonstrates any of the symptoms in this list, call your veterinarian immediately.

- Coldlike symptoms, such as coughing, runny nose or eyes, or fever

- Loss of appetite

- Lethargy or listlessness

- Loose stool alone more than once

- Bloody stool once

- Loose stool accompanied by other symptoms

- Vomiting alone more than once

- Bloody vomiting once

- Vomiting accompanied by other symptoms

- Enlarged joints or nodes

- Head shaking, walking in circles, or staggered gait

- Unusual excitability

- Unusual sensitivity to light or noise

- Convulsions or odd jerking movements

- Shortness of breath

- Excessive slobbering

- Abnormal posture or a hunched-up appearance

- Sudden appearance of a rash or skin lesions

- Any unexplained change in behavior or physical appearance

THE DOCTORED DOG

Some dogs with an upset stomach might not vomit, but they will try to crawl into your lap or sit on your foot in an uncharacteristic manner when they are in distress. An unusual walking pattern — staggering or walking in circles — could signal a neurological problem or tumor.

## How to Give Your Dog Medication

From time to time, you'll probably have to give your dog medication for treatment of a specific condition or perhaps as a preventive measure. If it's a pill, the easiest way is to wrap the pill in one of the dog's favorite treats, perhaps cheese, and give it to him. Some dogs, though, can't be fooled and will manage to eat the treat and spit out the pill. Another way is to crunch up the pill and put it in the dog's food.

If these methods don't work, you have to put the pill down the dog's throat, approaching from the side of the dog's mouth.

If you look there, you'll see that there's a space in between his teeth. Put a finger in, which will get him to open his mouth, so you can place the pill way back on his tongue — partially down his throat. Immediately shut the dog's mouth with one hand and rub his throat with the other, taking care not to cut off his breathing. If he didn't get the pill down, he'll spit it out, and you'll have to try again. Liquid medication can also be administered through that opening in the side of the dog's mouth.

Ask your veterinarian to give you a demonstration of how to pill the dog when he or she prescribes medication, just in case the dog won't eat it in his food.

If you need to administer topical medication — a cream or ointment to the skin — you'll want to make sure the dog doesn't lick it off before it's absorbed. Simply play with the dog or take him for a walk to keep him busy after application.

Never give your dogs pills intended for humans, such as antihistamines or aspirin, without checking first with your veterinarian. Although common household medications such as peroxide and antibiotic ointment are fine to use for minor cuts and scrapes on the skin, never use them in the dog's ears or eyes.

## The Old Dog

As your dog ages, you will notice behavioral and physical changes similar to those that occur in humans. There may be a decrease in activity, irritability, and even forgetfulness. The dog may be less tolerant of changes in the household, such as strangers visiting, than before. Her bones may ache, her skin and coat may lose some of their luster, she may be less tolerant of the cold, and she may not see and hear as well. She needs patience and tender loving care.

Fortunately, many of the problems that the elderly dog develops can be treated or minimized somewhat, and that's why you should be more diligent than ever about reporting any symptoms or changes in your dog to the veterinarian. The pain of arthritis might be relieved by some aspirin. If your dog has heart failure, diuretics and a special diet may help. Irregular heartbeats can be treated, just as they are in humans. If your dog has kidney problems, she probably needs more water — elderly dogs generally should drink more.

## Putting Your Dog to Sleep

*Euthanasia,* or putting your dog to sleep, is something to consider for dogs who are in so much pain that they are miserable most of the time, and when there is no prospect of making them better. Only your veterinarian can help you make the decision about whether it's time for euthanasia, which involves the injection of an anesthetic that causes loss of consciousness and painless death.

The emotions that dog owners experience at the loss of their pets are much like those experienced when a human loved one passes away. Expect to grieve — it is part of the healing process. Grieving for months or even longer over the loss of a dog is not unusual. Some owners find that they continue to hear the dog scratch at the door or make other familiar noises even after the dog is gone — this is normal, too.

It's generally thought that you should finish grieving for one dog before you go out and purchase another. But follow your heart. If you feel certain that bringing a new dog into the house will help fill the void left by the death of your former dog, do it.

The saddest scenario is one in which a pet owner refuses to get another pet. Some owners feel that they are betraying the pet that is gone, or fear having to live through the loss of a pet again. But someone once said that one of the greatest tributes there is to a beloved dog is to get another dog after he is gone — it is a way of saying that he brought you so much pleasure, it's an experience worth repeating.

## Pet Health Insurance

Health insurance policies for pets, similar to the traditional type of health insurance plans for humans, are available, but average dog owners might not find them particularly cost-effective. Guy Hodge, director of data and information for the Humane Society of the United States, says that the policies often exclude care such as routine immunizations and checkups, which probably account for a large portion of the average dog owner's bills. Some also don't pay for care required for genetic defects, such as hip dysplasia, or for treatment of injuries sustained at times the dog is considered to be improperly controlled by the owner. If you are interested in pet health insurance, Hodge advises you to "read those exclusions."

A newer type of health insurance for dogs is just emerging, one that would be worth investigating. It is prepaid health care, similar to health maintenance organizations (HMOs) for humans. In such a plan, dog owners join a clinic and pay a flat, usually annual fee that covers most dog health care, including routine preventive care. Ask around your area to see if such a plan is available. One drawback might be that such plans would pay only for care rendered at the participating clinic; if you're on vacation and your dog becomes ill or gets injured and you have to use another clinic, you may have to pay for the care yourself.

**CHAPTER 11**

# THE
# DOG HOUSE

*How to Keep Your House
from Smelling Like a Dog*

One of the most delightful things about puppies is the way they smell. It's difficult to describe, but it's a warm, cozy, pleasant odor. Somewhere alone the line, that pleasant puppy scent changes to a "dirty dog" smell. It's body odor from the dog, and even dogs generally thought to have no odor may begin to smell unpleasant if they are dirty. If your dog had an accident in the house that went unnoticed, it is sure to start smelling sooner or later. Before you know it, your entire home begins to smell like a poorly kept kennel. The odors become particularly prominent in humid weather.

But your house doesn't have to smell bad. First, keep your dog clean and well groomed. Then concentrate on keeping the odor out of your house, which you can usually do with ordinary household cleaning products.

Don't forget basic safety precautions: No matter how benign a household cleaning product seems to be, keep pets away from it, especially if you have a dog with allergies or sensitive skin. Use the products sparingly until you are certain they won't irritate the dog. Vacuum or rinse the products away thoroughly after use.

For products mentioned here that need special ordering, see the product information list in the back of the book.

## Finding and Eliminating Sources of Odor

Before you tear the entire house apart, consider whether there is one area that might be responsible for that dirty dog smell. Sometimes, though, a general house cleaning with special attention to areas the dog inhabits is the answer.

### The Dog Bed
This is a common source of odor. If it's washable, throw the dog's blanket or sleeping pillow into the washing machine. If the dog sleeps on something that isn't washable, try vacuuming it and then clean it with a nontoxic fabric cleaner; in the future, cover it with a washable blanket.

## Carpeting

Vacuum frequently to pick up dog hair and dander. One of the most inexpensive and effective ways to control odor in the carpet is to sprinkle the area with baking soda; leave it there for an hour or so, keeping the dog away from the area, then vacuum well. There are also dry, powderlike products made especially for cleaning carpets, and more and more people now have those home steam carpet cleaning devices, which generally work well. Do check with the carpet manufacturer's recommendations for how best to clean the kind of carpet you have.

You read in the chapter on housebreaking that urine accidents should be cleaned immediately with vinegar. But sometimes an accident goes unnoticed until the odor starts to permeate the house. Eliminating odor from these old urine spots can be difficult. If this is your problem, try the method recommended by Don Aslett in his book *Pet Clean-up Made Easy:* Use a bacteria/enzyme digester. If this alone doesn't work, wait four to six hours after application of the product and apply a solution of one cup white vinegar to a gallon of warm water. Rinse and apply the bacteria/enzyme solution again. Use enough to make sure that it soaks through to the carpet padding.

If you've found one old stain like this in the house, there are bound to be others; you might as well crawl around and sniff out the carpet to find other spots that need special cleaning.

If your carpet still stinks despite your best efforts, call in a professional cleaner, specifying that the problem is pet odors.

If your dog tracks everyday dirt onto the carpet, there's a product called Resolve, sold at grocery stores, that is very effective.

## The Vacuum Cleaner

If you notice that your carpet seems to stink primarily when you are vacuuming, the problem might be that the dirty dog smell is in the vacuum cleaner itself. Try wiping off the machine (with the cord unplugged, of course!), change the dirt receptacle or bag frequently, and try using a product called Breeze — vacuum cleaner deodorizer pellets that you put in the vacuum cleaner bag. It's available at grocery stores.

## Drapes

Drapes have a special affinity for collecting dog hair and dander and can really stink if not regularly cleaned. Vacuum them frequently, and have them washed or dry-cleaned as often as is practical and possible.

## Furniture

If your dog hangs out on your furniture, the upholstery may start to stink. Clean it according to the manufacturer's directions, but, for a quick cleanup, baking soda left to sit awhile, then vacuumed up, may help eliminate odor. If the dog leaves dirt on the sofa, try the product recommended above for carpets — Resolve — if it's safe for the kind of upholstery you have. It seems to work even on those greasy stains some dogs leave after rubbing their faces on the furniture.

# Dog Hair

If you have a breed that sheds heavily, the hair may contribute to odor, and it may be tough to keep it out of the house and off your clothes. It's also embarrassing to watch company leave your house with their entire backsides covered with dog hair because they sat on the couch.

Of course, the most obvious thing to do is to brush your dog frequently, which will reduce the amount of hair in the house.

Try to select furniture with sturdy, smooth fabrics that won't trap pet hair as easily as woven fabrics. Vacuum furniture and carpets frequently and sweep hard floors often to keep pet hair and dander to a minimum.

When you have a collection of dog hair, whether it be on your clothes or the furniture, rolls of heavy-duty tape made especially for removing pet hair work well. You can order them directly from the manufacturer by the case to save money.

If your dog is leaving hair around so heavily that even the heavy tape won't remove it easily, Don Aslett recommends using a pet hair rake.

# Dog Food

Unwashed dog food bowls and bits of dog food left lying around the floor can start to stink and will also attract bugs. It's a good habit to rinse out the dog's bowl with hot soapy water after each use. To keep food and water off the floor, place your dog's food and water bowl on a rubber mat or large towel that can be washed.

# PRODUCT AND INFORMATION LIST

For exercise pens and puppy playpens, call or write to:

Alpha Wire Products
P.O. Box 2371
Anderson, IN 46018
(317) 642-6088

Kong Company toys are probably available in your local pet supply shop. If not, write to the company for information:

Kong Company
300 S. Lamar Court
Lakewood, CO 80226

Nylabone products are widely available from pet shops, but if you can't find them, you can order directly from the company. Just be sure to mark your envelope, "ATTENTION: SMALL ORDERS":

Nylabone Corporation
Box 27
Neptune, NJ 07753

Pet hair pickups, those heavy-duty rolls of tape for getting pet hair off clothing and furniture, can be ordered in large quantities directly from one of the manufacturers. You're likely to find ordering in bulk cheaper than buying individual rolls at your local store. One supplier you can order from is:

Bemistape Division
2705 University Avenue, N.E.
Minneapolis, MN 55418

Pet car seats, pet deodorizers, dog door gates, winter coats, stool scoopers, the Doggie Dooley outdoor waste system for dog stool, and a wide variety of other pet products can be found in Pedigrees, a pet catalog. To obtain a copy, write to:

Pedigrees
15 Turner Drive
Spencerport, NY 14559-0110

KalMMusic, the tape designed to calm your dog, can be ordered from:

Starfire Enterprises
P.O. Box 3119
Warrenton, VA 22186

Having trouble with your building's pet policy? This organization has some pamphlets you may find helpful:

The Pet Food Institute
1001 Connecticut Avenue, N.W., Suite 700
Washington, DC 20036
(202) 857-1120

# RECOMMENDED READING

Here are just some of the many fine books available on dogs that you may find particularly useful:

*The Dog in Your Life* by Matthew Margolis and Catherine Swan, Susan McLellan, D.V.M., consultant (New York: Vintage Books, 1982). Besides basic information such as selecting and training a dog, this book has an excellent section on traveling with your pet. It features the sensible training methods of Mr. Margolis.

*Dog Owner's Home Veterinary Handbook* by Delbert G. Carlson, D.V.M., and James M. Giffin, M.D. (New York: Howell Book House, Inc., 1980). This book is an excellent source for learning more about the everyday health care needs and emergency care needs of dogs.

*The Evans Guide for Civilized City Canines* by Job Michael Evans. (New York: Howell Book House, Inc., 1988). Written by a man who left a monastery to take up dog training in the city, this book combines useful information for city dog owners with interesting autobiographical material.

*Harper's Illustrated Handbook of Dogs,* edited by Roger Caras; health care section by Robert W. Kirk, D.V.M. (New York: Harper and Row, 1985). Don't know a Puli from a Pekingese? You can find out in this book, which has beautiful color photographs and excellent descriptive information on various breeds.

*The Perfect Puppy: How to Choose Your Dog by Its Behavior* by Benjamin L. Hart, D.V.M., and Lynette A. Hart (New York: W. H. Freeman and Co., 1988). Over 50 popular breeds are featured as well as over a dozen behavioral traits for each, including which dogs snap the most, bark the most, and are the easiest to housebreak.

*Pet Clean-up Made Easy* by Don Aslett (Cincinnati: Writer's Digest Books, 1988). If you want detailed information on cleaning up after your dog and on special products available, try this book.

*Understanding Your Pet: The Eckstein Method for Pet Therapy and Behavior Training* by Warren Eckstein and Fay Eckstein (New York: Henry Holt and Co., 1986). This book is reportedly going out of print, but try to find a copy in your local library, especially if you are trying to determine the cause of problem pet behavior.

# INDEX

## A

Affenpinscher: owner profile, 22-23
Airedale: owner profile, 28-29
Allergies, 160-161
Anal sacs, 156
Animal control laws, 121-123
Animal shelter dog, 21

## B

Barking: and animal control laws, 123; problems with, 106-107
Basenji: owner profile, 26-27
Bathing, 129-132; full bath, 130-132; sponge bathing, 130
Beagle: owner profile, 26-27
Begging problems, 108
Behavior problems: in confined dogs, 102-108
Bichon Frise: owner profile, 22-23
Biting problems, 108
Bone and chew hazards, 79
Boston terrier: owner profile, 26-27
Boxer: owner profile, 28-29
Breeder's dog, 30
Breeds, 15
Brushing: of dogs, 127-129
Bulldog: owner profile, 26-27

## C

Cairn terrier: owner profile, 24-25
Car hazards, 85-87
Carpeting: and odor control, 170
Castration, 155-156
Charging the front door problems, 107-108
Chewing problems, 103-105
Chihuahua: owner profile, 22-23
Children: hazards with dogs, 83-85
Chin: owner profile, 22-23

Chow chow: as potentially difficult, 20
Christmas trees: and puppies, 51
Climate: and dogs, 18
Clipping and trimming, 129
Cocker spaniel: owner profile, 26-27
Collars: in obedience training, 94-95
Combing: of dogs, 127-129
Come command, 99-100
Commands: in obedience training, 98-101
Contact dermatitis, 160
Coprophagy, 147
Corgi (Cardigan Welsh): owner profile, 26-27
Crating method: for housebreaking, 58-62; pros and cons, 59-60; for puppies, 44
Cuts and scrapes, 156

## D

Dachshunds: owner profiles, 22-23, 26-27
Dalmation: owner profile, 28-29
Dane (Great): owner profile, 28-29
Dermatitis, 160
Diarrhea, 161-163
Difficult dogs, 20-21
Digging problems, 103
Distemper vaccine, 152
Doberman pinscher: as potentially difficult, 21
Dog bed: and odor control, 169
Dog beds, 44
Dog food, 143-144
Dog owner(s): personality and life-style, 11-14; selection of a dog, 9-35

THE GUILT-FREE DOG OWNER'S GUIDE

Dog selection: checklist for prospective owners, 32-33

Dog waste: and animal control laws, 122-123; Doogie Dooley, 70; feces cleanup, 68-70; indoor dog bathrooms, 65-69; puppy-proofing, 49-51; urine cleanup, 68

Dog(s): allergies, 160-161; animal control laws, 121-123; animal shelter dog, 21; barking, 106-107, 123; begging, 108; behavior problems in confined dog(s), 106-107; biting and nipping problems, 108; breeder's dog, 30; breeds, 15; castration, 155-156; charging the front door, 107-108; chemical dangers to, 75-78; chewing problems, 103-105; climate and, 18; coat, 17-18; crating, 58-60; crating method of housebreaking, 58-62; difficult dogs, 20-21; digging behaviors, 103; exercise and, 139-143; feeding of, 143-148; the first days at home, 39-51; first impressions in new home, 40-41; grooming, 127-136; growling, 123-124; health care, 149-166; house hazards, 73-81; housebreaking, 53-70; jumping up behaviors, 107; kennels, 116-118; large dogs, 16-17; lunging, 123-124; male vs. female in selection process, 19; nail grooming, 133-135; name samples, 48; new dog in the home, 39-51; obedience training, 89-108; odor control, 167-171; owner personality and lifestyle, 11-14; pet sitters, 113-116; pet store dog, 30-31; poisoning hazards, 75-79; puppy-proofing, 49-51; quiz for prospective owners, 10-11; schedules, 111-112; selection of, 7-35; and sleep areas, 44-46; sleep areas for, 44-46; small dogs, 15-16; space and 41-44; space for dog in house, 41-44; suburban vs. urban dogs, 10; talking to, 47-48; things dogs chew, 50; traits and personalities, 14-15, 31; visiting with, 124; waste and the law, 122-123; wetting, 46-47; whining, 46-47

Down command, 99

Drapes: and odor control, 170

E

Ears: ear-cropping, 153-155; grooming, 132

Electrical hazards, 74-75

English toy spaniel: owner profile, 22-23

Euthanasia, 164-165

Exercise, 139-143; indoor, 140-142; outdoor, 142-143

F

Feeding, 143-148; dog food, 143-144; foreign matter, 146-147; frequency, 145-146; treats, 146; vitamins, 144

Fetch and catch, 140-141

Fire hazards, 74-75

Fleas, 157-158; flea dermatitis, 160

Food poisoning, 77-78 Full bath, 130-132

Furniture: and odor control, 170-171

G

German shepherd: as potentially difficult, 20

Grass: eating of, 147

Greyhound (Italian): owner profile, 24-25

Griffon (Brussels): owner profile, 24-25

Grooming, 127-136; bathing, 129-132; brushing and combing, 127-129; clipping and trimming, 129; conditioning your dog for, 128-129; ears, 132; examining dog during, 129; and gum disease,

135; nails, 133-135; teeth, 135
Growling, 123-124
Gum disease, 135

**H**

Hazards: car, 85-87; children and dog(s), 83-85; household, 73-81; seasonal, 81-83; traveling, 87-88
Heal command, 100-101
Health care, 149-166; allergies, 160-161; anal sacs, 156; castration, 155-156; diarrhea, 161-163; ear-cropping, 153-155; euthanasia, 164-165; fleas, 157-158; insurance, 165; medication, 163; minor cuts and scrapes, 156; obesity, 157; old dog, 163-164; parasites, 157; poisoning hazards, 75-79; skin problems, 159-160; spaying, 155-156; tail-docking, 153-155; ticks, 158-159; veterinarian selection, 51-152; vital vaccines, 152-153; vomiting, 161-163; worms, 153
Hepatitis vaccine, 152
Herbicide hazards, 76-77
Home: and dog's space, 41-44; the first days, 39-51; first impressions, 40-41; new dog and other animals, 41
Hound (Basset): owner profile, 26-27
House hazards, 73-81; bones and chews, 79; electrical, 74-75; fire, 74-75; keeping the dog inside, 73-74; poisoning, 75-79; strangling, 74; toys, 79-81
Housebreaking, 53-70; crating, 58-60; indoor dog bathrooms, 63-67; newspapers for training, 63-64; odor control, 167-171; one-step method for puppies, 56-58
Household safety checklist, 84

**I**

Indoor dog bathrooms, 63-67; acci-dents, 66-67; cleanup of dog waste, 65-69
Indoor exercise, 140-141; "obedience" play, 141
Indoor kennels, 43-44
Inhalant allergies, 160
Insecticide hazards, 76-77
Insurance, 165
Irish terrier: owner profile, 28-29

**J**

Japanese spaniel: owner profile, 22-23
Jumping problems, 107

**K**

Kennels, 116-118

**L**

Large dog, 16-17
Leashes: in obedience training, 95
Leptospirosis vaccine, 152
Lunging, 123-124

**M**

Maltese: owner profile, 22-23
Miniature dachshund: owner profile, 22-23
Mounting problems, 108

**N**

Nails: clipping frequency, 135; and grooming, 133-135; nicking a vein, 134-135
Neutering, 155-156
Nipping problems, 108
Norfolk terrier: owner profile, 24-25
Norwich terrier: owner profile, 24-25

**O**

Obedience training, 89-108; behavior problems in confined dogs, 102-108; bullying, 96; commands, 98-101; housebreaking, 53-70; "obedience" play exercise,

141; owner expectations, 101-102; trainer selection, 92-94; training equipment, 94-95

Obesity, 157

Odor control, 167-171

Outdoor exercise, 142-143

Owners: dog owners' personality and lifestyle, 11-14

**P**

Papillon: owner profile, 22-23

Parainfluenza vaccine, 152

Parasites, 157

Parvovirus vaccine, 152

Pesticide hazards, 76-77

Pet sitters, 113-116

Pet store dog, 30-31

Pinscher (Miniature): owner profile, 24-25

Pit bull: as potentially difficult, 20

Plant hazards, 78-79

Poisoning hazards, 75-79

Poodles: owner profiles, 22-27

Prospective dog owners: quiz for, 10-11

Puppies: crates, 44; one-step method for puppies, 56-58; puppy-proofing, 49-51

**Q**

Quiz: for prospective dog owners, 10-11

**R**

Rabies vaccine, 152

Retriever (Golden): owner profile, 28-29

Retriever (Labrador): owner profile, 28-29

Rottweiler: as potentially difficult, 21

**S**

Schnauzer (Miniature): owner profile, 24-25

Schnauzer (Standard): owner pro-file, 28-29

Seasonal hazards, 81-83; cold, 82-83; heat, 81-82

Selection (of dog): factors influencing selection of a dog, 9-35; quiz for prospective owners, 10-11

Sheepdog (Shetland): owner profile, 26-27

Shih Tzu: owner profile, 22-23

Sit command, 98

Skin problems, 159-160

Sleep areas: for dog, 44-46

Small dogs, 15-16

Space: for dogs in house, 41-44; indoor kennels, 43-44

Spaniels: owner profiles, 22-23, 26-27

Spaying, 155-156

Sponge bathing, 130

**T**

Tail-docking, 153-155

Talking: to your dog, 47-48

Teeth: and grooming, 135

Terriers: owner profiles , 24-29

Ticks, 158-159

Toy fox terrier: owner profile, 24-25

Toy hazards, 79-81

Toy Manchester, 24-25

Toy poodle: owner profile, 22-23

Traveling hazards, 87-88

**V**

Vaccines, 152-153

Vacuum cleaner: and odor control, 170

Veterinarian: selection of, 151-152

Vitamins, 144

Vomiting, 161-163

**W**

Wetting, 46-47

Whining, 46-47

Whippet: owner profile, 28-29